LAPSIT SERVICES FOR THE VERY YOUNG II

A How-To-Do-It Manual

Linda L. Ernst

HOW-TO-DO-IT MANUALS
FOR LIBRARIANS

NUMBER 106

NEAL-SCHUMAN PUBLISHERS, INC.
New York, London

W9-CEH-128

Published by Neal-Schuman Publishers, Inc.
100 Varick Street
New York, NY 10013

The paper used in this publication meets the minimum requirements of American National Standard for Information Sciences—Permanence of Paper for Printed Library Materials, ANSI Z39.48–1992.

Printed and bound in the United States of America.

Library of Congress Cataloging-in-Publication Data

Ernst, Linda L.
    Lapsit services for the very young II : a how-to-do-it manual / Linda L. Ernst.
      p.   cm. — (How-to-do-it manuals for librarians ; no. 106)
    Includes bibliographical references and index.
    ISBN 1-55570-391-7
    1. Libraries—Services to toddlers—United States. 2. Libraries—Services to infants—United States. 3. Children's libraries—Activity programs—United States. 4. Public libraries—United States. I. Title. II. How-to-do-it manuals for libraries ; no. 106.

Z718.1 .E77 2001
027.62'5—dc21
                                     00-045076

For the very young beginning their life-long learning, and the adults who share the adventure with them.

CONTENTS

LIST OF FIGURES
IN APPENDIX C

PREFACE

"Lapsit" has become identified with public library programs and services aimed at serving the very young child, under two years of age, and their adult caregiver. They are created to foster positive interaction between the parent or adult caregiver and very young children in the area of language development and learning experiences. *Lapsit Services for the Very Young II* developed out of the latest research findings in the areas of how very young children learn, their language development, and brain research. *Lapsit II* is also intended to meet the need for more age appropriate programs and services to introduce very young children, ages 12–24 months, to the world around them.

In the early 1990s librarians began to expand their services to this very young age group and started offering regularly scheduled storytimes for the 12–24 month–old child. Lapsit programs quickly became an increasingly popular and expected area of service in many libraries. More and more, librarians have found themselves being called upon to present programs for the very young outside the library — at playgroup meetings, daycares, and even hospitals that have "new parent" groups.

I wrote my first book, *Lapsit Services for the Very Young* because of the need for a pathfinder to help librarians gain knowledge and expertise in their understanding of child development and selecting and developing age–appropriate programs. The first volume of *Lapsit Services for the Very Young* was written to help readers become more aware of child development and early brain research and provide the librarian with basic programs and services. It gave new-to-the-field professionals instructions on getting started and offered the more experienced resources and programs to expand their repertoire.

Lapsit Services for the Very Young II reflects the latest research findings and awareness of how early learning begins in life. It expands on the basic services, facilities, and programming librarians have begun to offer families with very young children. It also offers flexibility in programming with comprehensive lists of annotated age–appropriate books, rhymes, songs, and fingerplays. *Lapsit Service for the Very Young* and *Lapsit II* work as companion books but they can each stand alone.

This book can be used by the librarian, the early childhood educator, parent education teachers, childcare providers, and parents. Public librarians can use this book to develop and reinforce their own knowledge and expertise. Early childhood educators and care providers will find the text useful and timesaving when incorporating language and literacy components into their programs. As the importance of reading aloud to the very young becomes more widespread, parents, grandparents and other childcare providers continue to look for the best reading materials for this age group and how to use them. They will find the recommended book lists and activities simple to incorporate into their daily lives.

Lapsit II is divided into two parts. Part One, "Essential Background," supplies information regarding the latest findings in brain research and child development characteristics, descriptions of those who interact with the very young child, and ways in which libraries can serve this age group and their caregivers. Part Two "Program Building Blocks" describes the books and other materials that can be combined and used for actual programs where language interactions between the very young child and the adult take place.

The first chapter reviews the latest scientific research findings and what impact they have on libraries. Chapter Two gives detailed descriptions of how the very young child's physical, intellectual, social, and emotional development evolves with their language development. With a better understanding of very young childrens' developmental stages, the adults who interact with them on a daily basis will then be able to plan programs, development services, and interaction successfully. Chapter Three encompasses the various service areas such as staffing, facilities, collections, and outreach that a library may explore to reach the needs of this age group.

Part Two has been designed as a menu so that age-appropriate materials and activities can be selected in order to create customized original programs. It can also be used as a ready-reference to good books, rhymes, and activities to explore with an individual child. It contains the basic ingredients necessary to create a language learning experience between the very young child and adult, and all the essential elements necessary to create a lapsit program.

The material in "Program Building Blocks" includes:

- An annotated bibliography of over 130 books that librarians have successfully used with very young children. Bibliographic information, summaries, and a handy cross-reference to over 60 different themes are furnished for each title.
- "Nursery Rhymes and Fingerplays" provides an extensive sampling of the familiar and traditional in the genre. (Although most libraries will naturally own a variety of resources that feature many of these rhymes, I have assembled a wonderful assortment here for you in one place.) Each

entry is ready-to-use; verses complete with the corresponding gesturing instructions.

- "Theme Programs with Suggested Books and Rhymes/ Fingerplays/Songs," combines the best materials with appropriate themes.
- "Grab Bag Program" outlines ten different lapsit programs containing materials that create a 15 to 25 minute fun language experience for very young children and adults to take part in together.
- "Resources for Programming Ideas" supplies books and articles to develop the reader's own knowledge of program possibilities and available materials.
- "Enhancements" is the music section offering ways to add music to programs for singers and non-singers alike. The flannelboard section gives instructions on how to use this material in programs. The puppetry section contains suggestions on how to create one's own puppets or to purchase ready-made puppets.
- Recommendations for other activities include a playtime where the adult is given an opportunity to communicate and interact with the very young child.
- Appendix A contains the bibliographies for each section of the text in one central location so all the resources are available to facilitate locating materials on a given topic without "flipping through" the book.
- Appendix B gives acronyms and agencies along with their web sites for those agencies involved in early childhood learning.
- Appendix C supplies camera-ready handouts, suggested signage and program handouts to assist the presenter in preparation and as a starting point for their own ideas.

Why offer lapsit programs and services? We don't do it just because researchers or administrators tell us to. There are a variety of reasons ranging from philosophical and educational ones to those that are personal in nature. Lapsit programs and services are valuable introductions to the wonderful world of language in which the very young child and adult together share a fun, learning experience that they will then want to recreate. These experiences also encourage early brain development with verbal, visual and tactile stimulation. We have seen very young children become comfortable around language, books and, yes, even libraries and librarians. Language and learning becomes an integral part of these children's daily lives. As a wonderful side benefit, families attending lapsit programs often become regular library users. Creating child-friendly environments, collections, and services helps the library become an important part of the life of these very young patrons, the families with which they live, and the larger community. Parents and other adult caregivers gain confidence in their ability to share stories and interact more with their children. There are personal reasons as well for developing this area of service and programming. Seeing very young children's eyes lighting up, smiles brightening, and little hands clapping merrily along with a rhyme, song, or story makes me realize that sharing lapsit is one experience that no one should miss.

ACKNOWLEDGMENTS

A book such as this can only be created with the help of countless people willing to share their knowledge and expertise. All of the children's librarians and early childhood educators who share the stories, rhymes and songs in the public domain through the oral tradition, along with other adults who have kept these alive for new generations, deserve heartfelt thanks.

I am particularly grateful to the Children's Librarians of the King County Library System in Washington who allowed me to observe their programs, examine their collections, and who shared their ideas and concerns, and served as sounding boards for my ideas and concepts.

Thanks to Nancy Stewart of Friends Street Music for her willingness to share material from "Plant a Little Seed" and "Little Songs for Little Me" and allowing me to observe how she put these materials into practice. Thank you to the teachers at the Bellevue Community College PreToddler Lab at Enatai in Bellevue, Washington, for sharing their many resources and ideas, and supplying me with input from the early childhood educator's point of view.

To Michael Kelley and everyone at Neal-Schuman Publishers, and especially my editor Virginia H. Mathews, for her support, patience and determination to encourage the development of programs and services for the very young child, my thanks.

I'd like to acknowledge Flint Public Library in Flint, Michigan for permission to use material from "Ring A Ring O'Roses," Gospel Light Publications in Ventura, CA for permission to use one of their fingerpuppet designs from "Easy to Make Puppets" by Fran Rottman and Vachel Lindsay, authors of the poem/rhyme "The Little Turtle" (arranged in this text as "There was a Little Turtle").

My special thanks to my family and friends for their continuing support.

PART 1
ESSENTIAL BACKGROUND

1 BASIC FACTS AND "REVELATIONS"

WHAT WE KNEW

At the beginning of the twenty-first century, we are rediscovering some basic facts as well as uncovering some astounding revelations about the very young child. Early child development and brain research concerning the earliest years of life became the focus of much scientific research in the 1990s, when many researchers in psychology investigated whether it was "nature" or "nurture" that determined how individuals developed and lived their lives. "Nature" referred to the individual's genetic inheritance, "nurture" to the environment that surrounded the individual's rearing.

B. F. Skinner was a behaviorist who believed that all behavior was learned and could be modified by changing the environment. Change the experience, change the child. Jean Piaget was foremost in studying the cognitive development in children, believing that human consciousness and the thinking process influenced development. John B. Watson, considered the father of the school of psychology that became known as "behaviorism," stated:

> Give me a dozen healthy infants, well-formed, and my own specified world to bring them up in, and I'll guarantee to take any one at random and train him to become any type of specialist I might select—doctor, lawyer, artist, merchant, chief, and, yes, even beggarman and thief, regardless of his talents, penchants, tendencies, abilities, vocations, and race of his ancestors. (Bruno, 1992: 412)

Eric Erikson's psychological studies indicated everyone proceeds through eight stages of development from birth to death. All this research pointed to the profound impact of the earliest years of a child's life on future years, but could not resolve whether it was because the child was born inclined that way from birth (nature/genes) or the environment that was created for the child (nurture) determined the child's path in life. Some scientists believed the determining factor was children's genes or DNA, whereas other researchers stated it was the environment that had the most impact on how children succeeded down the road of life.

WHAT WE HAVE LEARNED

Now, thanks to a recent revolution in molecular biology and new imaging techniques, researchers believe that genes, the chemical blueprints of life, establish the framework of the brain, but then the environment takes over and provides the customized finishing touches. They work in tandem. The genes provide the building blocks, and the environment acts like an on-the-job foreman, providing instructions for final construction. (Kotulak, 1996: 3)

It is both nature and nurture together that create an individual who is well fitted not only to survive in the world but also to thrive.

In the past ten years, entire conferences and research reports have devoted themselves entirely to expanding the knowledge and awareness on topics concerning the very young child. National awareness has been increased by such events as the 1997 White House Conference on Early Childhood Development and Learning, The American Library Association's Presidential Paper in 1996–97 entitled "Kids Can't Wait . . . Library Advocacy Now" (based on many research studies by the Carnegie Corporation and others), and television programs such as "I Am Your Child" (*ABC Prime Time Special*, April 28, 1997) and *The Today Show*'s report (4/14/97) on "The Science of Child Development and the Brain." *Newsweek* devoted an entire special edition, the Spring/Summer 1997 issue, to the topic of young children, ages birth to three. *USA Today* included an article entitled "Brain Development Is Remarkable During First Few Years" in their August 1999 issue. *Time* ran a special report in the February 3, 1997 (vol. 149 no. 5) issue on how a child's brain develops. The article was entitled "Fertile Minds" and the issue included articles on what parents can do, as well as what some well known people are doing to support early childhood development.

The amount of information regarding brain development has become almost overwhelming for the layperson to absorb. This chapter supplies basic facts, research, and reports to give you an overview to early brain development and its impact on libraries and parents. It is important to remember that "the growing body of brain development research represents a multifaceted work in progress, and, as such, is not a singular nor completed study from which easy or simplistic conclusions can be drawn" (Puckett, Marshall, and Davis, 1999: 8–12).

In 1994, the Carnegie Corporation of New York released a report entitled *Starting Points: Meeting the Needs of Our Youngest Children* compiled by the Carnegie Task Force. It describes the "quiet crisis" that affects nearly half of the infants and toddlers in the United States. This group of children and their families face one or more of the following major risk factors according to *Building a Nation of Learners: The National Education Goals Report* by the National Education Goals Panel (1993):

1. inadequate prenatal care
2. parents that are isolated—divorced, single parent, those with less family and community support, those who themselves are undereducated
3. substandard child care—both parents working, high turnover and insufficient training for child-care providers
4. poverty
5. insufficient stimulation of children by caring adults

Libraries can help reduce these risks. By offering free programs, libraries can teach parents how to create a stimulating learning environment for their very young children, act as role models for parents in interacting with their children, help child-care providers incorporate this stimulation into their daily routines, and give parents/adults a chance to develop support networks with others.

New technologies and research tools have helped establish basic facts regarding brain development in the very young child. Children are no longer considered "blank slates" when they are born, waiting for stimulation. Prenatal studies show the fetus reacting to stimulation while still in the womb. The human brain is complex and vital to life, yet it is not complete at birth. It is the children's environments—what they eat, what they hear and feel, their sense of security, the interesting things around them—that impact how the brain connections develop.

BIOLOGY: THE FACTS AND "REVELATIONS"

Research shows that areas of the brain actively develop and mature at different times. This is why it is easier to learn certain things at certain times than at others. One example of this is in learning languages. *How Babies Talk* (Golinkoff and Hirsh-Pasek, 1999) provides an excellent explanation of how children learn the complex skills of language. Golinkoff also reinforces the importance of interaction between a child and an adult. Since children learn through all of their senses, it has been found that children have stronger connections between brain cells if they are held, touched, talked to, and played with on a regular basis by caring and involved caregivers. This is true of all children, be they hearing, hearing impaired, or those with special needs. Talking, language, and communication are all very complex things to learn, and it is critical for adults to take part actively in all aspects of a child's growing experiences. Repetition is important to reinforce what children experience. Communicating and demonstrating skills gives the child information as well as a role model to emulate, from using speech, to turning pages in a book, to any other skill the child is developing. Although children are born with an overabundance of brain cells and connections, over time it is only the ones that have active exchanges that survive. It is the old rule of "use it or lose it."

So what are the basic facts?

1. Children are born with 100 billion brain cells called neurons. There are 50 trillion connections or synapses functioning. This number increases the first few years of life, and then synapses that are not consistently being activated are "weeded out."
2. "Wiring" between the neurons increases significantly the first few months of life. However, pruning of unused synapses takes place over time.
3. Environmental factors have more influence on brain development than first thought, and they have a lasting influence.
4. A child's early experiences help determine the brain's "wiring."
5. The vitality of the connections is influenced by the child's environments and the amount of stimulation received. The connections between cells is strengthened through constant sensory stimulation.
6. Children's brains develop over time, with certain areas of the brain developing at different times and paces.
7. At three years of age, the child has about twice as many connections in the brain as an adult does.
8. There is a rapid rise in the number of synapses from 50 trillion to 1,000 trillion in the first few months after birth. (Carnegie Task Force, 1994:7)

When a child is born, the brain's major function is to sort out and become accustomed to the new world. By one year of age, the child is ready to seek new inputs. It is important to remember that each child is a unique individual who develops at a unique pace and in the areas that catch the child's interest. Yes, even at this early age, the young child displays definite interests and becomes a learning machine, though one limited by skills and abilities that need more time to develop. This will be examined more closely in the discussion of child development in chapter 2.

Helping children learn about themselves and the world around them is a primary responsibility of the parent and/or the primary adult caregiver. Learning about brain research can help adults guide children toward their full potentials by creating a stimulating, healthy learning environment. The research now being done indicates that children have the ability to learn even earlier than first believed. By using noninvasive methods and behavioral studies, data can now be gathered to trace electrical activity in the brain and note stimulants preferred by the child, such as sounds or pictures, through the study of sucking patterns.

"If parents spend the first year of their child's life worrying mostly about motor development, we devote the second to language" (Eliot, 1999: 351). Language is the main way people communicate with one another and learn about their world. Children develop this skill at different times, which often causes parental concern when comparing their child to others at the same age. It is through the experiences they have that children develop their primary language, be it English, Spanish, Hindi, or any other. The grammar and structure of the language, the richness and volume of its vocabulary, and how it is pronounced all need to be learned. Children are able to comprehend what is being said before they themselves have mastered the actual skills and abilities needed to talk. Eliot notes, "Learning to talk is probably the greatest intellectual leap of an individual's life: it opens up a new universe of questions, reasoning, social communication on opinions (for better or worse!) that punch all the other types of leaning into warp speed and make a child finally seem like a full-fledged person" (354). It is the foundation upon which intellect builds.

The world today needs people who are capable, confident, and competent in the areas of communicating and thinking. Technology, leadership, economics have become so global that mastering all aspects of communication is imperative. According to Golinkoff in *How Babies Talk*, the recent scientific discoveries regarding brain development and language show that:

1. Silence is *not* golden. Very young children learn through all of their senses. Communication is essential for language development, whether it be auditory (hearing) or visual (sign language). Television cannot be a substitute, since it does not demand interaction on the part of the child. A stimulating environment helps children remain interested in their world while learning about it. Interaction can be with the parent or an alternative caregiver. The important thing is engaging in communication with the child. Hearing-impaired children need stimulation as well. This can be done through the use of sign language, visual aids, touch, vibrations, and the like. Working class and professional parents talk more to their young children than welfare parents. Teen parents also tend to be unaware of the importance of talking to their child.

2. New scientific methods can yield assessment tools, such as methods for determining learning loss.

3. Overestimate your baby's capabilities, say the studies. They are learning more than you would suspect. Not only can little ones see and hear, but they are also analyzing and remembering experiences. (Golinkoff and Hirsh-Pasek, 1999:142)

IMPACT ON THE LIBRARY

With all that this "early brain research" is revealing, what implications does it have for libraries and librarians? The Idaho Library Association states: "As members of the early childhood education community, librarians play a crucial role in applying what is known about brain research to their own libraries and in helping educate parents about the role they play as their children's first teacher" (*www.lili.org/isl/rlbrain.htm*). Librarians have the ability to empower parents, no matter what their economic level, to be the best teachers they can be (not teachers in the formal "school" sense, but motivators, horizon-openers rather than just instructors), to help them create an environment that gives their child a good start to lifelong learning. It is also important for librarians and early childhood educators to be aware of conflicting interpretations of brain research by researchers. Terms such as "windows of opportunity" can be misinterpreted and cause parents to have unrealistic expectations for their children or cause them to overreact to generalizations. "Parents need assurance that the window does not close on a child's third birthday" (Puckett, Marshall, and Davis, 1999). In fact, what many parents enjoy doing naturally with their children, such as touching, talking, singing, and playing, is essential "food" for the brain.

How does the library respond to the latest scientific research? Libraries have increasingly emphasized the importance of reading aloud for the entire family, including the very young child. Librarians can be guides and role models for parents and caregivers on what and how to read to children; how to talk about characters, experiences, and situations; and how to create a stimulating environment for enjoyment and then learning to take place.

America's librarians who serve children and families know a wonderful secret that spurs them on despite budget cuts and staff shortages. They know that every time they share a story or a book, a game or song, with tiny children—infants, toddlers, or energetic three to five year olds—and their young mothers and sometimes fathers—

they have a chance to light a flame of perception or a memory that will remain with a human being forever, and may even make a difference in an entire lifetime. (Mathews,1996–97: 7)

Libraries and librarians can be teachers and role models for helping to build the foundation for the literacy skills a child will develop when school age and will use throughout life. Moving beyond the traditional library patron, librarians are offering story times for younger children and holding instructional workshops for the adults who live and work with children, and by collaborating with other agencies in the community to reach the nonlibrary user. Libraries are striving to be a true developmental resource for children and families—whatever their cultural origin or economic background—during their vital early learning years.

How can libraries spread the word? How can libraries better link their capabilities and resources to the importance of language in the early part of a child's life? First, understand the participants involved: the adult caregiver and the very young child. Next, determine what plan is the most efficient for working with this group in a particular situation. For example, there may be in-house programs—that is, programs in the library—networking with other agencies in the community to find participants. This requires organizing in-house resources for better accessibility, creating a more child-friendly environment (including changing areas), and presenting workshops for teen parents or other specific groups. Explore who is involved, what materials should be used, and where these services should be offered. Some programs may be offered in sites other then the library—sites that may be easier for mothers/primary caregivers to get to.

Science had shown the importance of language in the early years of a child's life. There are ways the librarian, early childhood educator, and caregiver can provide language education through our services and programs. Part II of the text provides program building blocks. Let us first look at the services other than programs that can encourage language development in very young children.

RESOURCES ON BRAIN RESEARCH

BOOKS

Bruer, John T. *The Myth of the First Three Years: A New Understanding of Early Brain Development and Lifelong Learning.* New York: Free Press, 1999.

Bruno, Frank J. *The Family Encyclopedia of Child Psychology and Development.* New York: Wiley, 1992.

Carnegie Task Force on Meeting the Needs of Young Children. *Starting Points: Meeting the Needs of Our Youngest Children: The Report of the Carnegie Task Force on Meeting the Needs of Young Children.* New York: Carnegie Corporation of New York, 1994.

Eliot, Lise. *What's Going on in There? How the Brain and Mind Develop in the First Five Years of Life.* New York: Bantam, 1999.

Golinkoff, Roberta Michnick, and Kathy Hirsh-Pasek. *How Babies Talk: The Magic and Mystery of Language in the First Three Years of Life.* New York: Dutton, 1999.

Gopnik, Alison, Andrew N. Meltzoff, and Patricia Kuhl. *The Scientist in the Crib: Minds, Brains, and How Children Learn.* New York: Morrow, 1999.

Healy, Jane M. *Your Child's Growing Mind: A Guide to Learning and Brain Development form Birth to Adolescence.* Rev. ed. New York: Doubleday, 1994.

Kotulak, Ronald. *Inside the Brain: Revolutionary Discoveries of How the Mind Works.* Kansas City: Andrews and McMeel, 1996.

Staso, William H. *Brain under Construction: Experiences that Promote the Intellectual Capabilities of Young Toddlers.* Book 2 of a series: *6–18 Months.* Orcutt, Calif.: Great Beginnings, 1997.

ARTICLES

"Brain Development Is Remarkable During First Few Years." *USA Today* (August 1999): 8–9.

"Brain Research Finds and Suggested Actions." *Oregon's Child: Everyone's Business,* Straight Shooting Exhibit, Oregon State Capital (February 1997).

Clinton, Hillary Rodham. "Comfort and Joy." *Time.* Special Report (February 3, 1997). Available online at: *www.time.com/time/magazine/1997/dom/970203/special.comfort_and.html*

Marcus, David L., Anna Mulrine, Kathleen Wong, and Deanna Lackaff. "How Kids Learn." *U.S. News & World Report* (September 13, 1999): 44.

Mathews, Virginia H. *Kids Can't Wait . . . Library Advocacy Now!* President's Paper written for Mary R. Somerville, president, 1996–97, ALA.

Muha, Laura. "Your Baby's Amazing Brain." *Parenting* (fall 1999): 40–45.

Nash, J. Madeleine. "Fertile Minds." *Time*. Special Report (February 3, 1997). Available online at: *www.time.com/time/magazine/1997/dom/970203/cover0.html*

Puckett, Margaret, Carol Sue Marshall, and Ruth Davis. "Examining the Emergence of Brain Development Research: The Promises and the Perils." *Childhood Education* (fall 1999): 8–12.

Ressner, Jeffrey. "Hollywood Goes Gaga." *Time*. Special Report. (February 3, 1997). Available online at: *www.time.com/time/magazine/1997/dom/970203/special.hollywood.html*

Simmons, Tim, and Ruth Sheehan. "Brain Research Manifests Importance of First Years." *News & Observer* (February 16, 1997). Available online at: *www.news-observer.com/2little2late/stories/day1-main.html*

"What Parents Can Do." *Time*. Special Report (February 3, 1997). Available online at: *www.time.com/time/magazine/1997/dom/970203/special.boxes.html*

"Your Child From Birth to Three." *Newsweek*. Special Edition (spring/summer, 1997).

WEBSITES

www.nncc.org/wh/whconf.html
The White House Conference on Early Childhood Development and Learning. April 17, 1997. Contains links to other Websites on the latest in brain research.

www.nccic.org/cctopics/brain.html
National Child Care Information Center. Provides an overview of the resources available. Lists publications in addition to organizations and links to information on brain development in infants and toddlers for parents and caregivers (does not endorse listings).

www.hpl.lib.tx.us/events/hdr_index.html
Houston Public Library's 1998 Harriet Dickson Reynold Program "BabyThink: Babies Belong in the Library" page. Has extensive list of Internet links covering fact sheets, articles, libraries, and programs, plus organizations, including the American Library Association, that relate to brain development and other areas concerning the very young child and the library.

www.nap.edu/html/sor
National Research Council containing report from the Colorado Department of Education "Starting Out Right: A Guide to Promoting Children's Reading Success" (ISBN 0-309-06410-4). Print version available though the National Academy Press (800-624-6242). Online at *http://stills.nap.edu/html/sor*.

www.lili.org/isl/rlbrain.htm
Libraries Linking Idaho's Brain Development page. Includes implication of such research for librarians, parents, and caregivers; facts and links for more information about brain development. Excellent bibliography listing brain development materials.

www.iamyourchild.org
I Am Your Child homepage. Information about brain research, child development of ages zero to three years, resources, and more.

www.naeyc.org/resources/eyly/1997/11.htm
National Association for the Education of Young Children. Early years are learning years: what it means for young children and their families.

www.ecnewsnet.org
Chicago Early Childhood News Network–Brain Research. *www.ecnewsnet.org/brainlinks/html* supplies links to the following: Early Childhood Initiative at the University of Chicago, Erikson Institute, Zero to Three Infant Development and Education, Society for Research In Child Development, San Francisco Early Childhood Information System Network.

www.nncc.org
National Network for Child Care. Serving professionals and families who care for children and youth. Select "Information Station," next "Child Development," then "Brain Development."

www.governor.wa.gov/early/home1.htm
The Governor's Commission on Early Learning. Gov. Gary Locke, state of Washington. January 2000.

www.brainnet.wa.gov
BrainNet. Early brain research development for parents, caregivers, policy makers. Includes information on partnerships, and resources. Great site! WA Child Care Resources & Referral Network and WA Dept. of Social and Health Services with additional private partners. 1–800–446–1114

2 WHO IS INVOLVED

CHILD DEVELOPMENT

The baby sleeps, wakes, cries, is fed and changed, observes the world for a moment, then falls asleep again. The pretoddler picks up a board book, tastes it, puts it back down, then repeats the process. Not much learning going on—or so it seems to the uninitiated. The connections in the brain are multiplying and working full speed through repetition and experience, so learning is almost always happening within a child. An understanding of child development helps you understand how much and how constantly children are learning about themselves and the surrounding world. It also helps if the adult has a fairly realistic concept of the child's abilities, skills, and needs.

How can one learn to plan programs that will help create the appropriate stimulus for a child to learn, and what kind of program is appropriate? There are different ways to become educated in this field. You can go to school, be it for a single college course or series toward a degree. Or you can take advantage of hospital offerings on the topic of mental and emotional development available in your area, or educate yourself through the "public university," otherwise known as the public library. As an active promoter of emerging literacy experiences for the very young child, librarians need to know about child development so they can help educate adults with very young children on how to create a stimulating learning environment on their own. Librarians should function as the experts—in how to read aloud, what to read aloud, the benefits of reading aloud to the very young child— but it takes more than merely demonstrating how and what to read to the very young child. Our work includes conversing, encouraging children to imagine, to put their own words to pictures and link their own experiences and feelings to words. In short, we help children learn to derive meaning that relates to them from words and pictures, and we assist parents and other adult caregivers in doing these things. We are not, however, the experts in supplying diagnoses or evaluations of individual children. We fulfill these needs by directing the adults to information sources, support groups, and the experts who can assist them. We need to understand not only the little ones but the adults involved in their lives as well.

To keep things simple, I define the various age groups in the following manner:

infant	birth to 12 months
pretoddler	12 to 24 months
toddler	24 to 36 months

preschooler   ages 3 years to 5 years
adult   the parent or caregiver who has significant contact with the child at the program or elsewhere

The term "lapsit" pertains to ages 12 to 24 months. This period covers a wide range of developmental stages and of various abilities of the child. Some children are still observing their world from a static position, while others have discovered their mobility, and still others are ready for the "Me do!" of toddlerhood. The pretoddler child is "in between" the infant's total dependency on adults and the toddler striving for independence (Ernst, 1995: 26). Ready to venture out into the world, the pretoddler still requires strong and immediate connection with the primary caregiver. This is why the adult is such an important participant in this program. The child and adult form a partnership that helps the child with language-acquisition efforts (Soundy, 1997).

Physically, the large motor skills are developed and mastered first by children. That is why little ones have more success with large movements such as moving their entire arm than with fine motor skills such as finger movements. For example, the "Eentsy Weentsy Spider" is easier for them to act out if it is changed to "The Great Big Spider," since they can use their whole bodies instead of trying to control only their fingers. Manipulation of objects can be practiced with large objects such as chunky crayons.

Between the ages of 13 and 18 months, the child's brain starts to connect sounds, symbols, and concepts to the physical world. Children in this period can follow simple instructions such as "Bring me the book" or "Stop." They are beginning to name and identify objects. Body gestures and simple one- or two-word sentences begin to help the child communicate, but verbalization is still limited: They can comprehend more than they can verbalize. Attention spans are short. It is within this time period when most children begin manipulating, conquering, and learning the skills necessary to exist in the physical world around them.

From 18 to 24 months, pretoddlers start to be much more in control of large motor skills and able to do more with the physical world around them. They can jump on two feet, get up stairs, and explore their fine motor skills. This is also when they concentrate on language and communication. Many children this age face a lot of frustration due to their lack of ability to verbalize what they are feeling or want to know. This frustration can lead to insecurity on the part of the child. They are developing speech and language skills more rapidly at this age than at any other, however, and have a vocabulary of about twenty words or more. The child this age needs extensive exposure to language, which can be accomplished through conversations with the caregiver; by listening to rhymes, songs, and stories; and by creating conversations with toys or even themselves. They need to constantly experience and practice with language.

It is important for the adult to understand the child's method of communicating. This can be done by "reading" the child's body language. Crying, turning away, wiggling, loss of eye contact, and even falling asleep will let the adult know the child has had enough for now. Smiles, babbling, and gestures can be interpreted that things are going well. Some basic sign language has even been taught to the very young, the use of which seems to relieve some communication frustrations. By giving the child time to examine and contemplate what is going on around them, an adult can make learning language skills a positive experience. Brief conversations, looking at one picture or page in a book, reciting a rhyme at bathtime or the bedtime ritual of a lullaby incorporate these mini language learning experiences throughout the child's day.

Encourage adults to use the following when communicating with children through stories, play, or everyday activities:

- *C*—Comment on what the child is doing, and then wait. Give the child time in which to respond, at least five to ten seconds. Describe or make a statement about what is happening.
- *A*—Ask questions. What is it? What happens next? What is that? Then wait. Remember children's minds may be in high gear but they also *need time to process their thoughts*. It is important for the adult to give them this time, so wait for their reply.
- *R*—Respond, add a little more to what the child says. Help by rephrasing what the child says. By doing this, the adult can demonstrate the proper use of language and give the child the example of a complete sentence. For instance, if a child were to say "truck," the adult would reply, "Yes, it's a big truck."

CAR (comment, ask, respond) comes from the Washington Research Institute's *Language Is the Key* video series. This method is best employed one on one but can be demonstrated in a group session by using lift-the-flap books and other participatory books.

The child will often concentrate on one specific skill that takes priority over others for a period of time. This will cause other skills to recede for awhile. This usually happens until that specific new skill is mastered and is incorporated into the child's daily life. This is all part of the child learning how to be a separate individual, which is a challenging and sometimes scary venture. This means the child will look to the familiar caregiver for support and reassurance. Separation anxiety is apparent when the child is put in an unfamiliar situation or with strangers. Maintaining familiar routines, environments, and people, however, will help the pretoddler gain confidence and mastery of the surrounding world.

THE CHILD—DEVELOPMENTAL STAGES, AGES 12 TO 24 MONTHS

At this age, the very young child is developing a real personality that is facing many first-time events. At this time, children seem to absorb everything around them. This is a time period not only of rapid physical growth but also of skill mastery for the child—skills that will last a lifetime. In a sense, children of this age can be described as "learning machines," and most adults will agree that the switch is always on!

The developmental stages for this age group will be looked at in two separate groups: the 12 to 18 month old, and the 18 to 24 month old. Each age group will be described by its physical development, intellectual and language development, social and emotional development, the specifics of which provide ideas and keys to responses from the adult caregiver.

AGES 12 TO 18 MONTHS
Physical Development
Large Motor Skills

- Can stand and sit alone.
- Crawls.
- Can bend over and pick things up.
- Can go up and down stairs—up by holding onto someone or something, and down by backing down the stairs on their knees.
- Throws a large ball with two hands, and can also roll it.

Fine Motor Skills

- Can carry objects when walking.
- Can push push-toys and cars along.
- Gestures or points to indicate things.
- Turns pages in a book but not individually.
- Loves to sort and dump things from containers.
- Scribbles using whole-arm movement.
- Thumb and forefinger pincer grasp gaining competency.
- Waves bye-bye.
- Starting to use spoon.

Intellectual and Language Development
- Has a vocabulary of 10 to 20 understandable words.
- Imitates others (words).
- Understands simple commands—one-step directions.
- Starts to name and identify objects.
- Comprehension development ahead of verbalization skills.
- Prefers the familiar.
- Very sensory oriented—feel and touch.
- Babbles, incorporating real words and sounds.
- Begins to identify parts of body.
- Books are still toys.
- Uses language to get adult's attention.

Social and Emotional Development
- Separation anxiety apparent when separated from parent or other primary caregiver.
- Plays alone.
- Enjoys being held and read to, security.
- Imitates others (actions).
- Showmanship: likes to have an audience and applause.
- Prefers individual, one-on-one attention.
- "MINE"—starts to claim own possessions and space.

Ideas for Adult Caregivers
- Play with the child preferably at his or her level. Peek-a-boo, rolling a ball, dramatic creative play such as making believe you are going shopping.
- Give the child a chance to develop ability to play alone independent of adult.
- Provide sensory experiences for the child such as playing with playdough, water, paint, or crayon. Use large enough surfaces, since hand-and-eye coordination is still being developed.
- Select books that will be interesting to the child and that have sturdy pages. Read stories that contain familiar objects, simple story lines that often reflect child's daily routine.
- Talk to your child; engage in conversations and give the child time to respond.
- Supply materials that can be sorted and put into containers. These can include cards in a dishpan, clothespins put into a coffee can, and the like.
- Relax and have fun with your child in various situations such as dancing to music, telling a story or nursery rhyme while changing a diaper, and describe what you are doing.
- Give lots of support and reassurance that you, the adult, are there for the child (hugs and verbal expressions).

AGES 18 TO 24 MONTHS
Physical Development
Large Motor Skills

- Can kick large ball.
- Can jump with two feet together.
- Starting to run.
- Pulls pull-toys.
- Climbs on and into things, such as boxes.
- Can walk up and down stairs with assistance.

Fine Motor Skills

- Able to throw smaller balls.
- Can build towers out of three to four blocks.
- Scribbles on paper, more vertical action.
- Begins to manipulate objects such as puzzle pieces to fit in required space.
- Can use a spoon without help.
- Turns knobs.

Intellectual and Language Development

- Vocabulary has grown to several hundred words.
- Points to body parts and can identify.
- Identifies pictures of objects and can name them.
- Starting to overcome obstacles such as opening a closed door.
- Can follow two or three simple directions.
- Remembers routines and patterns.
- Likes to echo people or repeat things.
- Starting to show preferences in making choices.
- Time being noticed in such ways as "now" and "later."
- Likes to "read" or tell story to adult.
- Still inventing words and learning rules of grammar.
- Asks questions, lots of questions!

Social and Emotional Development

- Still has difficulty sharing.
- Self-centered.
- Likes to take short walks.
- Will play alongside other children doing the same thing (parallel play).
- Independence starting to show ("No!").
- Wants everything now.
- Tries to do things without assistance.
- Can get physically aggressive when frustrated.

- Enjoys listening to stories, songs, and rhymes.
- Memory is still not developed.
- Likes to play pretend, imitating what is seen in the surrounding environment (telephone conversations, for example).
- Can separate from parent/adult easier in a familiar setting.
- Likes to "read" stories, turn pages—explore books.

Ideas for Adult Caregivers
- Continue talking to your child and encouraging participation in the conversation.
- Do not constantly correct the child's speech.
- Read to your child at least fifteen to twenty minutes a day.
- Make rhythm instruments and dance to music.
- Encourage pretend play by providing clothes, mirror, scarves, and similar items.
- Expand on what your child says using the CAR method.
- Supply writing/drawing materials.
- Create an environment where you and your child are comfortable with and open to learning experiences that happen all around you.

For more ideas on how the adult can support the very young child, see the section on activities in chapter 5.

THE ADULT

Now that we have a better understanding of very young children and how the adult can support them, what about the adults? How can understanding adults help us create services and programs? The child does not grow in a vacuum. It is imperative that a caring adult act as a guide and participant in the child's life. It is necessary for the very young child's brain to be stimulated in order to develop and grow. This can only be done when someone or something creates a positive developmental climate for the child.

The term "adult" in most cases will refer to the parent. These can be first-time parents, experienced parents, teen parents, working parents, low-income parents, undereducated parents, or parents who speak another language than English. If not a parent, then the adult is someone who cares for or has major ongoing responsibility for the child. It may be one of the more than four million grandparents who have taken on this responsibility or had it thrust upon them. Whoever the adult may be, all the adults have one thing in common: they want the best for the child. They may not understand, however, how essential it is to share experience with children.

Parents today find themselves being pulled in many directions. Stress levels are often very high, and some parents place almost unbearable pressure on themselves regarding their child's development. Many other parents may not be aware of the importance these few months have on the rest of their child's life. "Welfare parents talk less to their toddlers than do either working-class parents or professional parents. According to the observational data, the average welfare child heard only 616 words per hour, the working-class child, 1,251 words per hour, and the professional child, 2,153 per hour" (Golinkoff and Hirsh-Pasek, 1999: 142). Parents for whom English is a second language (often referred to as ESL), may have reservations about their ability to speak English to their child or feel self-conscious when they do so. Teen parents may have difficulty reconciling their new role as parent to that of being a teenager. Grandparents are often the ones doing day care and are unsure of what to do with the very young child in regard to today's standards. Many parents feel pressure because they want to "do it right" and at the right time, but sometimes are not even sure of what "it" is. They create their own tension, which needs to be minimized before the child can have a healthy and stimulating environment in which to learn and grow.

Sometimes the adult may simply need to be reminded and educated about child development. Simple basic "to do" ideas help to emphasize that child's play is actually work. Adult caregivers need to be made aware that what children experience will influence their self-identity and social wellness as well as what they will learn and how they will grow. Emphasize to the adults how important it is that they:

1. Read to their child at least fifteen minutes a day. It does not have to be done all at one time or even all from the same material. Read recipes, stories, the paper, grocery lists—any and everything! Include songs and rhymes to add variety.
2. Incorporate books into a daily routine such as bedtime or after a meal.
3. Use eye contact to involve the child, especially during language experiences such as when doing rhymes, songs, and the like.
4. Be a role model for the child. Let the very young child see how books are held, pages turned, and other habits. Children should see the adult reading books and magazines and newspapers of interest. Sturdy board books and old catalogs will help children practice these skills. Children are copy cats at this period!
5. Make the experience fun. Be expressive in your reading aloud, and allow the child to interact with you.

6. Use the public library. Economics as well as space considerations do not allow for everyone to have an extensive home library. Adults need to know what materials can be borrowed at the public library, how the library can direct them to needed services/agencies, and that there is no charge for these services. Borrowing library materials is also a good way to sample books, audio material, or videos before purchasing. Children most often want to possess a much-loved, often-read, favorite book.

7. Make sure the child is in an environment that will be a creative, stimulating learning experience for them. Day-care providers need to interact with the child, not just feed and change diapers. Remember also the brief attention span that the very young child has, and be prepared to adjust to it.

8. Give the child time to respond. Enthusiasm is wonderful, but the adult needs to remember that the child's brain needs time to process and absorb what is happening before responding.

THE SPECIAL NEEDS FAMILY

Most of the information given is geared to the average family, but we cannot dismiss any group that does not match the definition of "average." The special needs family, multilingual families, those in shelters or other housing, and teen parents all need special support for giving their children the best possible environment in which to learn. All families of diverse kinds should be respected—not only for their differences but also for their similarities to the "average" family.

Mainstreaming has become the norm in the public schools, and the public library is required by law to provide access for children with special needs to attend programs, as stated in the Americans With Disabilities Act, 1992. Statements that reflect this fact are often included on program flyers indicating that would-be library users should notify the library if special accommodations need to be made. More often than not, however, special needs children do not attend public programs, therefore special outreach programs need to be created in order to serve this group. Check in your area telephone book or directories for listings of local chapters of national organizations, hospitals or health centers that may have parent support groups, and others to which you may offer this service. Some suggestions are: mental health centers, community health centers, societies for the blind, Easter Seals, programs for developmental delays, community service centers, social services agencies, and specialized schools. Librarians sometimes are uncomfortable with this service due to their possible lack of experience and training in the area of special needs. The most important thing to remember is that in many ways all children are identical in their needs: They all need touch, security, attention, and exposure to developmental and language-building experiences. Librarians can connect through the agencies in their community or offer workshops on the importance of reading to the very young for the teachers at special needs schools and agencies.

It can sometimes be challenging to select material for special needs groups. Often you can use the same material as for the "average" child, but you need to be aware that you may need special material or some assistance. For example, enlarged pictures may assist you during a program for visually impaired children. Presenting a story program for deaf or hearing-impaired children would benefit if the librarian/presenter could use sign language or enlist the aid of an interpreter. You may need more tactile material such as flannel-board stories, Braille books, puppets, movable books, and the like.

Accepting the children and interacting with them as they are is vitally important. Parents of special needs children are often already very involved with their child. The presenter's ability to be relaxed while displaying a positive attitude will let the adults know that sharing books and building a language-learning experience should be part of their children's lives just as it should be for other young children.

The following lists some simple program ideas that help strengthen certain skills the children have by using fingerplays, rhymes, and songs. For words and directions, see chapter 4.

1. Practicing standing and balance:
   - Pop Goes the Weasel can involve standing upright, hopping, and turning.
   - Hickory, Dickory Dock involves standing upright, bending, and clapping.
2. Helping develop visual tracking:
   - Two Little Black Birds uses flannel-board pieces that are placed on a board and then moved, or puppets that change location.
   - Roly Poly uses a puppet when demonstrating putting it in the appropriate location such as "up," "down," and other directions.
   - Humpty Dumpty can be used for visual tracking of up and down movements.
3. Sitting upright:
   - 1,2,3,4,5, I Caught a Fish Alive gives the child brief moments of sitting independently, which is reinforced with a positive hug.
4. Naming parts of the body:
   - Head and Shoulders, Knees and Toes
   - These Are (child's name) Fingers
5. Musical activities: include dance and movement so the child and adult have positive interaction with sounds, rhythm, and movement.
6. Large flannel pieces children can place on flannel board: "Lots

of Cars," a song from *Plant a Little Seed* by Nancy Stewart, is an example of what works well. Make simple car shapes in bright felt colors that the children can put on the flannel board themselves with minimum assistance from their caregivers.

7. Use lots of repetition and rhyme: *Brown Bear, Brown Bear* by Bill Martin is a good example.

8. Encourage touch between the adult and child using interactive rhymes, fingerplays, and songs.

9. Often puppets help bridge the gap between presenter and participants: "Here Comes a Mouse" from *Catch Me and Kiss Me and Say It Again* by Clyde Watson can be used with a mouse puppet, which can give the child a little tickle.

Resources for the Special Needs Child

Feinberg, Sandra, Kathleen Deerr, Barbara Jordan, and Michelle Langa. *Including Families of Children with Special Needs: A How-to-Do-It Manual for Librarians*. New York: Neal-Schuman, 1998.

Greenspan, Stanley I., and Serena Wieder, with Robin Simons. *The Child with Special Needs: Encouraging Intellectual and Emotional Growth*. Reading, Mass.: Addison Wesley, 1998.

Library Service to Children with Special Needs Committee, Association for Library Service to Children. *Programming for Serving Children with Special Needs*. Chicago: American Library Association, 1994.

Wright, Kieth C., and Judith F. Davie. *Serving the Disabled: A How-to-Do-It Manual for Librarians*. New York: Neal-Schuman, 1991.

THE BILINGUAL FAMILY

American society is enriched by the many cultures brought together to create it. It is important that these various cultures be respected and preserved. Some children hear their parents speaking only in their native language at home, some adults cannot read English, and some adults live secluded from the community. The librarian must be knowledgeable and aware of different cultural norms when serving the bilingual family. In order to have a successful program, the presenter may need to have a good command of another language or work with an interpreter. Immigrant families that attend programs for the lapsit age group can benefit in various ways.

1. They are exposed to simple vocabulary, story lines, and other material in English, which they sometimes recognize as being related to those from their own background. Sharing similar fingerplays is a good way to share cultures.

2. Their children are nonjudgmental and love the language-sharing experience, so the adult has a positive experience reading

English aloud. Besides, if the library can also supply material in the native language, the child will have two language experiences.

3. Reading simple stories and repeating rhymes aloud will give adults practice using the English language.
4. The adult has an opportunity to network with other adults, which they may have not had before.
5. The adults can be made aware of bilingual material and services they can then take advantage of. If you have bilingual stories in your collection, make sure you display them and direct the families to their location. Reading a story in English and then having the same story available in the patron's native language builds a bridge many will cross. If you plan to use your usual English materials remember to speak clearly and slowly but naturally. Demonstrate with words and action, use visuals, and most importantly, relax and smile to put your participants at ease.

Those involved with teaching English as a foreign language often use anagrams such as ESL (English as a second language) and EFL (English as a foreign language). *The EFL Playhouse . . .* is a Website resource for teachers of young learners that has an excellent link page connecting to many ESL- and EFL-related sites for fingerplays, language resources, teaching tips, and so on. Their Internet address is: *http://members.tripod.com/~ESL4Kids/links.html.*

TEEN PARENTS

Teen parents are often accessible through vocational schools, alternative high schools, welfare centers, health clinics, Head Start centers, and other child-care facilities. Teen parents need information about basic child development, parenting strategies, and other demands that are being placed on their lives. Quite often they have no idea of the importance and role that language and interaction play in their child's life. If teens did not have the childhood experience of adults who read aloud, it is very likely they are not readers either. The librarian can become their role model. Since childhood for them is not in the distant past, some may remember favorite stories, songs, and rhymes. They need to be encouraged to share these with their child. Teen parents often respond well to hands-on experiences. Programs for the very young child enable them to do just that and to learn themselves as they teach their child.

GRANDPARENTS

As we have indicated, there are more and more grandparents taking on the role of full-time or part-time child-care provider in the past few years. This group of adults needs the support of the public library. Often with limited resources, grandparents can find the library's lapsit programs a way for the very young child to have a social and educational experience. The library can also support them as they try to help the child in this new contemporary world, so different from when they were parents. Refreshing their memories of stories, rhymes, and songs from their past, and educating them to the new information and research regarding the importance of the first few years of life, helps the grandparent in many ways. Parenting strategies they once firmly believed in may get shaken. "Don't pick the baby up, you'll spoil him" has given way to the realization that little ones need the physical closeness of a caring adult. Grandparents did not have the current child-development information available when they were new parents, and they need to learn how children develop and learn. Grandparents may also be able to spend more time interacting with the child in order to create a stimulating learning environment and a better chance for future success in school and in the work world than they or their children had.

CONCLUSION

Programming for the very young requires you to address a great variety of audiences. Many levels of development can be apparent in the children that attend the programs. Adults are varied in their background and in their needs. How do they all fit together? In general, programming for the 12-to-24-month-old child group is divided into two groups, but sometimes this is not possible. If both age ranges are mixed in one group, some of the adults attending may compare and worry about their child. My response has always been to reassure the adult. The 12 to 18 month old may not actively take part in the program, but if the adult will do so then the language experience, especially when repeated at home with the adult, will become part of their everyday life at home. The 18 to 24 month old can take a more active role in the language experience and will share that with the adult caregiver. The entire age range benefits by the stimulation received through interaction with the adult, which helps strengthen brain connections and helps develop children's skills and emotional responses. Each child proceeds through experiences at a unique pace. The adults will grow in their desire to share with their child a positive experience when they see how easy and common-sensical it is. Lapsit programs are designed to enjoy but not just to entertain. They serve to empower and educate the parent/adult caregiver with simple activities so the adult and child get off to a good start toward developing the child's full potential.

RESOURCES FOR CHILD DEVELOPMENT

BOOKS

Ames, Louise Bates. *Your One-Year-Old: The Fun Loving, Fussy 12–24 Month Old.* New York: Dell, 1982.

Bos, Bev. *Before the Basics: Creating Conversations with Children.* Roseville, Calif.: Turn-the-Page Press, 1983.

Caplan, Frank and Theresa. *The Second Twelve Months of Life.* New York: Putnam, 1977.

Eisenberg, Arlene, Heidi Murkoff, and Sandee E. Hathaway. *What to Expect: The Toddler Years.* New York: Workman, 1994.

Ernst, Linda L. *Lapsit Services for the Very Young: A How-to-Do-It Manual.* New York: Neal-Schuman, 1995.

Golinkoff, Roberta Michnick, and Kathy Hirsh-Pasek. *How Babies Talk: The Magic and Mystery of Language in the First Three Years of Life.* New York: Dutton, 1999.

Herb, Steven, and Sara Willoughby-Herb. *Using Children's Books in Preschool Settings: A How-to-Do-It Manual for School and Public Librarians.* New York: Neal-Schuman, 1994.

Hobbs, Sylvia. *Parent Handbook for Pretoddler Observation Class.* Bellevue, Wash.: Bellevue Community College, 1987.

Kutner, Lawrence. *Toddlers and Preschoolers. A Parent and Child Series.* New York: William Morrow, 1994.

Mathews, Virginia H., and Susan Roman. *The Library-Museum Head Start Partnership.* Washington, D.C.: Center for the Book in the Library of Congress, 1999.

Nespeca, Sue McCleaf. *Library Programming for Families with Young Children: A How-to-Do-It Manual.* New York: Neal-Schuman, 1994.

Van der Zande, Irene. *1,2,3 . . . The Toddler Years: A Practical Guide for Parents and Caregivers.* Santa Cruz, Calif.: Toddler Care Center, 1993.

VIDEOS

Washington Research Institute. *Language Is the Key: A Multilingual Language Building Program for Young Children. Talking and Books* and *Talking and Play.* Produced by the Washington Research Institute with Mary Maddox, Kevin Cole, and Angela Notari-Syverson. 20 minutes. Washington Research Institute, 1998, rev. 1999. Two videocassettes and manual. Currently available in English and Spanish, soon to be available in additional languages. For more information call (206) 285–9317 or online at *www.wri-edu.org/bookplay*

WEBSITES

www.nncc.org
> National Network for Child Care. This site has an "Info Station" that will direct you to articles, resources, and other links.

www.iamyourchild.org
> The "I Am Your Child" homepage.

www.nccic.org/cctopics
> National Child Care Information Center. Covers child-care topics.

www.naeyc.org/naeyc
> National Association for the Education of Young Children. "Children's Champions" links to many other sites.

www.ala.org/alsc/teachers.links.html#development
> The American Library Association, ALSC Division. Has sites for teachers, parents, and librarians. This address connects directly to the list of sites for child development.

ARTICLES

Soundy, Cathleen S. "Nurturing literacy with infants and toddlers in group settings." *Childhood Education* (spring, 1997): 149–153.

3 SERVICE AREAS

Serving the 12 to 24 month old and caregiver needs to extend beyond programming alone. Library in-house services should include facilities, staff, and a collection that is appropriate for this age group. Libraries also often create their own outreach programs to respond to the needs of their communities, or they can tie into national or local program offerings by networking with outside agencies, both public and private.

In examining all the possibilities, you can often become overwhelmed and feel responsible for library services that seem to be growing exponentially. The library needs to be able to evaluate its in-house as well as its outreach services to see how they meet the need in your community. The staff must also know the needs and characteristics of its community before beginning services. This chapter will help simplify things and direct you in this area. It will also demonstrate that the librarian does not have to do it all alone.

IN HOUSE

In house is often the best place to begin serving this clientele. Services include staffing, the physical area and layout, collections, and any "extras" your library/school or care facility can provide. Let's look at each of these issues separately.

STAFFING

Staffing has a strong impact on the amount and kind of services that can be offered. A professional who has training and experience in children's library services and some background in child development has the best chance of fairly easy success. This person would be familiar with the developmental stages and needs of the child, be knowledgeable in children's literature, and have the ability to interact positively with not only the child but also with the adult that accompanies that child. Awareness of patron needs and their possible misgivings about going to the library, however, needs to pervade the entire staff. Help the nonprofessional and other staff who don't usually serve the children by keeping them informed so that they can create a welcoming and friendly environment for child and adult. Make sure the staff is aware of the educational and lifelong impacts such programs have on these children's lives. Often lapsit programs are looked at—especially by those not directly serving children—as just fun time, but it is much more: it is "purposeful enjoyment." Helping the rest of the staff understand that one of the purposes for this program is to develop readers and library users in the coming years can help build understanding and strong support for children's services within the staff.

PHYSICAL AREA AND LAYOUT

The actual physical area and layout influences how this clientele is served. Is it an age-friendly place as well as being as child safe as possible? If there is a separate parenting area, it should be close by the children's section, since children should not be left alone even if it is "just for a moment" while the adult looks for a book or parenting information. Are the books for this age group accessible by the children? Since many of the books for this age group are board books, can the children reach them, sort through them, and replace them? It may look neater with all the books lined up on the shelves, but if the child can't reach the books, what good are they? In fact, it is likely the child may climb the shelves in an attempt to reach them, which is dangerous. Eye level and reachable are concerns that need to be considered when organizing these books. For example, board books can be placed in colorful plastic boxes or crates, or placed in book racks that can be left on low tables.

Look at your area to see if it is appealing and encourages reading experiences between the child and adult. There are various kinds of chairs that can encourage the pair to cuddle up or share a story. Comfortable stuffed chairs, rocking chairs, soft foam chairs such as beanbag chairs, and pillows can suggest this. For some facilities, large pieces of furniture might be possible such as a playhouse or a giant stuffed toy to lean upon. Although it is nice, it is not necessary to have even a special chair or object. A reading spot can be created by adding a bright rug sized to fit your available area.

Remember, too, to establish changing areas in both the men's and women's washrooms. Not too many adults want to stay in the vicinity of a smelly diaper. Making changing tables available helps the adult realize that their child is welcome in the library too.

Decorations

Posters are often useful for decoration. Bright, colorful, story-related posters are wonderful, as are those that have children in them—children love to look at photos and illustrations of other children. The new Redmond Library in Redmond, Washington, for example, has huge photos of individual children from around the world. They immediately spotlight who this area in the library is devoted to and welcomes them. You can also add interest to this area by attaching bright pieces of fabric to a wall and draping and overlapping them. For example, by using various colors of chiffon, you can drape the pieces so that a new color is created where they overlap.

In addition to a child-welcome and -friendly environment, remember to make sure the area is also a safe one. Check regularly for sharp or small objects that might find their way into little mouths. Cover electrical outlets with safety covers (available at many grocery, department, and hardware stores). Keep cords away and out of the reach of inquiring fingers. Sharp corners can also be cushioned with foam or commercially available plastic bumpers.

COLLECTIONS

The collection holds the treasures that children and adults seek. Make sure there is a good representation for books suitable for ages 12 to 24 months (recommended titles can be found in chapter 4). Board books are essential, since children this age have not yet developed the fine motor skills necessary for turning pages in a book. Fingerplay books and audio materials add depth to the collection's ability to help the adult expand the language experience beyond the verbal and visual by encouraging the child to hear, see, touch, and act out the words. By hearing the words, seeing illustrations, responding to what they hear with actions, children become immersed in the world of language; all these sensory experiences reinforce perceptions and concepts to help develop communication skills. Some libraries use colored dots to identify books that are age appropriate. This assists the adult looking for material suitable for a particular age. Have a key to dot colors clearly visible.

Five characteristics of books appropriate for this age group are:

1. sturdy pages that can handle rough usage without ripping
2. illustrations that are clear, bright, and colorful; children this age enjoy looking at pictures/illustrations of other children
3. sized to fit in the child's hands
4. brief text and simple plot; many reflect the child's daily activities or experiences
5. white space on the page, which gives the child a sort of "rest spot" and also a chance to examine and absorb what is actually there

The demand on collections by child-care providers and educators can often be high. It can therefore be to your advantage to prepare other ways of presenting or packaging the collection. For example, Washington's King County Library System maintains a *Books to Grow On* collection, which consists of age-appropriate books, curriculum ideas, adult support material, and some type of enhancement, be it a puppet, appropriate toy, or the like. These groupings are "theme kits filled with surefire books to read-aloud, cassette tapes, videos and other materials on a variety of curriculum topics." These kits are aimed at the very young and are very popular with child-care providers, teachers, and busy parents. An offshoot of this, *The Books to Grow On for Toddlers* kits, is designed for children two years old and younger. The kits cover such topics as "My Body," "My Day," "Animals," and "Things That Go." Originally intended only for day-care providers, *Books to Grow On* and *Books to Grow On for Toddlers* kits are now available to the community and circulate very well among the families throughout King County.

Collection guides are another useful in-house service. These usually consist of printed materials such as booklists, publicity flyers, activity sheets, support materials for parents, and so forth. Examples include:

- recommended titles that are age appropriate for the very young
- lists of board books, concept books, and other categories
- nonprint materials recommended for children, and how to use them, on topics such as music or movies
- parenting skills and concerns, which can be language related or general in nature and include reading aloud to children, discipline, toilet training, anger management, know your one year old, sibling rivalry, and the like
- activity sheets such as fingerplays, music books, and crafts that the adult and child can use at home to create a language experience
- Titles to help the adult who works with children on topics such as fingerplays, music, child safety

Other handouts can be publicity flyers for age-appropriate programs, how and what to read aloud, reasons to read to your child, and topics such as how to select a child-care provider/playgroup for your child, safety awareness, or Internet safety (see Appendix C for sample handouts). Libraries are usually very willing to share what they know and have created, so remember to check around your area to see what may already be available. Many times conferences are a good place to "swap and shop" ideas and materials with others in the field. Professional handouts may also be obtained by contacting various local organizations such as local health clinics, day-care and preschool sites, and ESL support groups, as well as national organizations. Five well-known organizations are:

1. American Library Association
   50 East Huron Street
   Chicago, Illinois 60611
   800–545–2433
   www.ala.org

2. The Center for the Book
   Library of Congress
   101 Independence Avenue SE
   Washington, DC
   202–707–5221
   www.lcweb.loc.gov/loc/cfbook
3. Children's Book Council
   568 Broadway
   New York, New York 10012
   212–966-1990
   www.cbcbooks.org
4. National Association for the Education of Young Children
   1509 16th Street NW
   Washington, DC 20036
   202–232–8777
   www.naeyc.org
5. Reading Is Fundamental, Inc.
   600 Maryland Avenue, SW, Suite 500
   Washington, DC 20024
   202–287–3220
   www.rif.org

EXTRAS

It is important to think of possible things that can be offered in your facility to increase the child-friendly atmosphere and enhance the language-learning experience you wish to create. Things that help develop skills for reading and language work wonderfully. A soft stacking toy has been a nice addition to the children's area in our library; children can enjoy it without creating too much noise, and can practice sorting, eye-to-hand coordination, and manipulating. Throughout this play they also hear language from their interaction with the adult who is speaking to them. Puzzles containing few pieces, perhaps only four to six, are fun and give the child a sense of accomplishment upon completion. Puppets and dolls encourage imaginary play and storytelling—not only by the child but by the adult as well; many times I have seen a puppet be the instigator of dialog between adult and child. Having in-house material beyond board books may not even be that much of an extra luxury. A little one putting a puzzle together or interacting with a puppet or toy is less likely to be pulling all the books off the shelf, unintentionally creating some concern and distraction for the accompanying adult and the staff. The relaxed adult is more likely to have the time to see the wonderful collection and services the library provides. The more relaxed, safe, and welcomed the adult feels when entering your facility, the more likely that person will be willing to return again with the child.

OUTREACH

As we well know, not everyone in the community is a reader or library user. Staying within the confines of our walls and creating wonderful in-house services and programs is what some might call "preaching to the choir." On the whole, library programs and collections are used by those who know about them and have the inclination to take advantage of them. It is the nonlibrary user and nonreader that we need to reach with the message about how important the library is to a child's first few years of life. We need to reach this population with the message that the library can help to bring about interaction between the very young child and a caring adult and help supply the language-building experiences during the first years of a child's life. But where do we find this group? Who would benefit from our services and expertise? What should we offer as outreach services, and where do we get assistance in this venture?

WHERE ARE THEY?

Where do we look for a population that needs library services but doesn't seem aware of their needs and those of their very young child? Child-care centers, parent-support groups, Early Head Start programs, family child care, hospital and health care clinics are all good places to start. If the community has housing projects or low-income housing, immigrant-support centers, and alternative high schools, other populations come into view. Community colleges will sometimes offer childhood observation classes for adults and the very young child. Find out if there are long waiting lists for these services and programs; if there are, this will give you an idea of the need in your area. This proved true for the Newport Way Library in Bellevue, Washington. Bellevue Community College in Bellevue, Washington, offered a wonderful pretoddler observation lab that exposed the very young child and adult to a wonderful and enriched, fun learning experience. The waiting list for this program was extensive. Newport Way Library developed an evening lapsit program that was offered numerous times throughout the year and met some of the community's need (see Ernst, 1995, for more information on this series). A target audience can be found by checking in the local yellow pages, with the state child-care licensing department, with social service agencies, or with other education and child-development organizations to determine area needs. Conferences for child-care providers and early childhood educators also provide another way of locating people who would benefit by connecting with the library. Groups that might be interested in working with the library include:

- child-care centers
- professional associations
- parent-education groups
- Head Start and Early Head Start sites
- family-support agencies
- relocation centers
- hospitals, pediatricians, and health providers in clinics
- early childhood educators

WHO ARE "THEY"?

Outreach services for the most part need to be aimed at a specific group. Most of us would like to reach everyone, but, with limited staff and resources, it is necessary to set priorities and determine a target audience—for example, parents with very young children. Teen parents can be reached very often through vocational or alternative schools. Families new to the United States often attend ESL classes or visit agencies that can support them as they relocate and settle in their new home. Some communities may have migrant camps where helping the adult and very young child discover a new world of language may influence not only the child but also the entire family.

Teachers and caregivers of the very young are a very important target group as well. Libraries can enlist this group to help build pre- or emerging-literacy experience by teaching the day-care teachers/care providers how to create language programs on their own. A library that provides workshops and talks on how to make reading a significant part of children's lives before formal schooling and reading instruction begin can help ensure learning success in school. Other agencies also need to be informed of the importance of early language building; an important one is WIC (Women, Infants, and Children centers), which serves parents of very young children. Service clubs, Rotary clubs, community-service agencies, and others can often provide assistance such as funding for a special outreach collection to travel outside the library. The more people involved in reading to the very young children and aware of the importance of interaction between the very young child and adult, the greater the potential there is for the very young children in your community to develop to the best of their abilities.

Once a target group is decided upon, you need to connect with them. When doing so, it is essential that *we not assume anything*. Many people have no idea of what a library is or does, what it has to offer, or the many resources it makes available to the community. Just the fact that one can borrow a book and take it home might amaze some people. Keep a conversational tone throughout your presentation. When meeting with these various groups, the simpler the program presentation, the better it is received. The target audience will need handouts to help them create the language experience on their own, since it is often difficult for people to travel to the library. Among low-income families, transportation is often an almost insurmountable obstacle.

WHAT CAN WE OFFER?

Since outreach implies "going out," be careful to evaluate your resources such as the collection, staffing needs, and other services already in place before extending a service or program that cannot be supported. Some services may demand time to create before physically being out of the building. Others require not only time to create but also time and staff at another location other than the library. Some programs may be part of a series, while others are a one-time event. Professional librarians may be the only qualified presenters for certain programs, whereas volunteers might be trained to do other programs. There are many options for outreach. Let's explore the possibilities.

Possible Outreach Services

Newsletters are a useful way of informing people about the library's materials and services. They require time to write and develop, as well as time to create mailing lists, actually get printed out, and prepared for mailing. Information regarding the very young child's developmental stages, books to share with them, or ways to enhance the language-learning experience can all be possible topics for such letters. Developing a mailing list of those involved with the very young child, sending these letters to child-care agencies and even to pediatricians or health clinics will keep people aware of the library, and how it's reinforcing their objectives.

Community events can also spread the word that the library is for little ones. Some hospitals hold whole-day events or "fairs" that sometimes focus on such topics as health, parenting family resources, and children. By hosting a table or booth at one of these events, the library can display its materials and services for the very young and provide handouts. Other such events take place in malls and at various sites in the community, but no matter where they are, they are an opportunity to reach out to the nonlibrary user. These are all opportunities to remind adults such as parents, caregivers, early childhood educators, doctors, nurses, and others that the library is part of their team to help children develop to their highest potential.

Another option is to create a collection that can be left at a site for use by the very young child and adult. Sites can include Early Head Start centers, child-care centers, well-baby clinics, pediatricians offices, and shelters. Setting up these books, which would be for use while the adult and child are at that location, also allows the librarian to connect with the director and teachers when collections are replenished or rotated and thus create a networking connection. Since it is difficult for sites with large staffs to get to the libraries, having the library come to them is often very appreciated. An example of this service can be found at the Multnomah County Library in Oregon, which offers a child-care center program. Picture-book collections are placed in private and public child-care centers and Head Start programs on a rotating basis.

Book "give-away" programs for new babies can let people know little ones deserve books and should be read to. They can also increase the library's popularity. Cost, however, is a major factor with this program, so outside support may be needed to help finance it. Many, if not most, of the programs like this have been aimed at populations that include many nonusers. The child receives a board book upon leaving the hospital, or gets a coupon for a free book, redeemable at the local library. The "Read Me a Story" program, for example, was funded by the King County Library System, the Bellevue Friends of the Library, and Overlake Hospital Medical Center in Bellevue, Washington. It includes a bib that has "Read Me a Story" printed on it, a coupon redeemable for a free board book at the Bellevue Regional Library, and a flyer that covers such topics as reasons to read to your baby, making time for reading, where to read, and some suggested rhymes and songs. (For more information, contact the Outreach Librarian for the King County Library System at 426–369–3323, or the Bellevue Regional Library at 426–450–1775.) Many libraries have adjusted the target age for programs like this to the "older" child, say twelve months or more; such programs also have an impact on the child's life. There is more interaction between the adult and child at this stage of development.

Offering workshops for early childhood educators and child-care providers enables the librarian to enlist more people to promote early foundations for literacy and the importance of the early mental and emotional development years. Workshops may cover (1) introduction to library services and materials, (2) how and what to read to very young children, and (3) how to incorporate the language-learning experience into the daily routine. Other possible topics for workshops might include ones that support the child-care and education-certification requirements for child-care providers and early-childhood educators. Library materials and their use, for example, are included in the National Official Child Development Associate curriculum guidelines for certification as a Child Development Associate, though you should investigate what the requirements are to be a qualified instructor. Hosting such courses is an option, where the library can be the location for such classes and programs that outside instructors teach. In any case, the librarian has the opportunity to spread the word that reading to the very young and conversing with them about books is important and that the library is available to assist in the venture. For example, Multnomah County Library in Oregon offers a variety of educational programs on such topics as "Beginning with Books" and "Born to Read" for parents, and programs on early-childhood resource training for centers and family child-care providers about six times a year. (For more information contact Early Childhood Resources, Multnomah County Library, 205 NE Russell Street, Portland, OR, 97212, 503–248–5458.)

You can also use story programs for outreach. This enables the participants to have an actual role model on how to read to children, what kinds of materials to use, and what activities encourage reading; actual program outlines can be found in Ernst (1995) and Nespeca (1994). Locales for such programs can include:

- social service agencies
- food banks
- shelters
- development centers
- alternative school—teen parent classes
- health clinics
- welfare offices
- correction facilities
- migrant camps
- Head Start/ Early Head Start sites
- ESL centers or relocation centers

Many times, these programs are presented by the librarian. This can place a high demand on the librarian's time, and in-house services could be disrupted. To counter this, volunteers can be trained on how to present such story programs and thus increase the availability of this program without placing additional stress on the staff. Multnomah County Library uses trained volunteers for its "Books While You Wait" program which takes children's books to waiting rooms in agencies where parents and children are waiting for medical or social services. Multilingual materials are included in this program.

Outreach programs have been created by private and national organizations that local libraries can also take advantage of. Although there are costs involved with these programs, the components have already been designed and created, thus saving time and costs in the long run. Many of these programs are for infants rather than the 12-to-24-month-old child, but if you have to start somewhere, these may be the best options in a given situation. Following are a few of the program offerings, along with other organizations that might be of interest in the areas of outreach. A list of agencies and organizations that you might look into partnering with is given in Appendix B. Your area's yellow and white pages along with checking Sandra Feinberg and Sari Feldman's book *Serving Families and Children Through Partnerships* (Neal-Schuman, 1996) may give you additional agencies/organizations to investigate.

- Born to Read: How to Nurture a Baby's Love of Learning.
  The American Library Association/Association for Library Service to Children
  Designed to instill the joy of sharing books with children by parents, child-care providers, teachers, and other adults. Various materials available, including a video and training manual. Librarians and health providers partner for this program. For more information, check the Website at *www.ala.org/alsc.*
- Reach Out and Read: A National Pediatric Literacy Program Fostered by the Department of Pediatrics at Boston Medical Center
  Pediatricians encourage parents to read aloud to their young children, and the family receives free books with pediatric checkups from six months to five years of age. Some programs partner with libraries. For more information contact:
  Reach Out and Read
  2 Charlesgate West
  Boston, MA 02215
  617–638–3380
  www.reachoutandread.org
- Center for the Book in the Library of Congress
  This was created in 1977 by an act of Congress to stimulate public interest in books, reading, and libraries and to encourage the study of books and print culture. It has thirty-six state affiliates, with a wide variety of programs. The center administers a family-literacy project in rural southeastern and southwestern states, providing grants from the Viburnum Foundation, workshops, and year-round consultation to grantees. Also a national program, initiated by an affiliate:
  Beginning with Mother Goose
  Vermont Center for the Book
  256 Haywood Road
  Chester, VT 05143
  800–763–BOOK
- National Center for Family Literacy
  325 West Main Street, Suite 200
  Louisville, KY 40202–4251
- Family Place Project
  Project of Libraries for the Future, in partnership with the

Middle Country Public Library. Model for programs, services, and collections that have been developed for parents, caregivers, and professional serving families. For more information on the Parent/Child Workshop, contact:

Family Place Project
101 Eastwood Boleveard
Centereach, NY 11720–2745
631–586–0303
www.mcpl.lib.ny.us/familyplace.htm

- Early Head Start
Early Head Start National Resource Center
This site is operated by Zero to Three: National Center for Infants, Toddlers and Families and WestEd's Center for Child and Family Studies. Zero to Three is a national, nonprofit charitable organization whose mission is to strengthen and support families, practitioners, and communities to promote healthy development of babies and toddlers. For more information, contact them at:

734 15th Street, NW, Suite 1000
Washington, DC 20005
202–638–1133
www.zerotothree.org

- America Reads Challenge: Ready*Set*Read for Families
A joint project of the Corporation for National Service, the U.S. Department of Education, and the U.S. Department of Health and Human Services. Has early childhood language activates for children from birth through age five.

- Reading Is Fundamental, Inc.
Provides books free of charge for children from infants to age eleven, but books must be provided by shared local funding. More information is available at:

600 Maryland Avenue, SW, Suite 600
Washington, DC 20024
800–RIF-READ
www.rif.org

RESOURCES

Ernst, Linda L. *Lapsit Services for the Very Young: A How-to-Do-It Manual.* New York: Neal-Schuman, 1995.

Feinberg, Sandra, and Kathleen Deerr. *Running a Parent/Child Workshop: A How-to-Do-It Manual for Librarians.* New York: Neal-Schuman, 1995.

Feinberg, Sandra, and Sari Feldman. *Serving Families and Children through Partnerships: A How-to-Do-It Manual for Librarians*. New York: Neal-Schuman, 1996.

Feinberg, Sandra, Joan F. Kuchner, and Sari Feldman. *Learning Environments for Young Children: Rethinking Library Spaces and Services*. Chicago: American Library Association, 1998.

Lenser, Jane. *Programming for Outreach Services to Children*. Chicago: American Library Association, 1994.

Nespeca, Sue McCleaf. *Library Programming for Families with Young Children: A How-to-Do-It Manual*. New York: Neal-Schuman, 1994.

Trotta, Marcia. *Managing Library Outreach Programs: A How-to-Do-It Manual for Librarians*. New York: Neal-Schuman, 1993.

PART 2
PROGRAM BUILDING BLOCKS

4 THE PLAY'S THE THING!

Programming for the pretoddler or 12 to 24 month old has become standard for many libraries throughout the United States. Parents are increasing their demands for it because of their desire to give their children the best and earliest start possible for developing mental, social, and language skills. In return, libraries are striving to serve the whole family and have discovered that serving this age group encourages many families to become regular library users. Using this service as an outreach program such as to teen parents, non-English speaking groups, and others often draws in nonlibrary users by appealing to the adult's desire to benefit the child and share experiences through either entertainment or education—which are one and the same for the small child.

Another benefit from programming for the very young is that the adult has an actual role model demonstrating what and how to read aloud to and communicate with their child. By being expressive, adding appropriate sounds, varying the length of the story and talking about the pictures, the librarian encourages the adult to do likewise. Learning about and seeing quality books that are age appropriate for their child gives the adults confidence to select books on their own. Reading aloud to the child also enables the adult to practice reading skills and gain competence.

Many parents/adults are so often overwhelmed with the primary needs of day-to-day life that reading to their children often falls by the wayside. Librarians can demonstrate how and when reading aloud and developing imagination, curiosity, and language skills can fit into everyday living experiences inside and outside of the home.

GENERAL FORMAT

The average length of programs for the 12-to-24-month age group is twenty to thirty minutes, but this can be expanded by allowing time before and after the class for participants to interact. The presenter should have enough material prepared to allow for flexibility in the program. A very active group may need more action rhymes and songs, a quieter group may be able to listen to more stories. Once the presenter gets started, it may be tempting to extend the duration of the program—everyone seems to be having so much fun! My advice is: Don't do it! Children this age can become overstimulated, and you do not want the experience to become a crying, chaotic mess.

The lapsit program described in *Lapsit Services for the Very Young* (Ernst, 1995) was set up as a series. Much of it can be adapted as well to either a weekly program or a one-time program. The four basic sections remain the same.

Part 1: Setting the Stage
Part 2: The Story Time
Part 3: Parent Education
Part 4: Bonus

PART 1: SETTING THE STAGE

This is the time to create an atmosphere in which the adults can relax and become familiar with the group. It is sometimes useful to let participants introduce themselves, their children and the ages of the children. Knowing this, the presenter can tailor the program to the proper age group. Adults tend to compare their own child to others in a group setting; having an awareness of the age range may relax this. Simply stating at the start that each child is unique and developing at a unique pace may defuse to a degree the tendency to compare.

Name tags are optional, although at times they may become a distraction, especially for the children. Address labels are often the best bet: They are not very decorative, but by putting a simple sticker or stamp at one end they serve the purpose well. Ask the adult to make two tags: one with both the adult's and child's names, the other with the child's name. Stickers fascinate children, and in order to prevent the tag from becoming a distraction simply put the tag with the child's name on the child's back.

Adults are often as new to this kind of experience as the children. If you give some guidelines, they can be reassured as to expectations of behavior and activity so they can relax and enjoy the program. These guidelines can be presented in one of three different ways:

1. Simply state the guidelines to the group at the beginning of the program.
2. Write them clearly on a poster, which then can be displayed at each program. Direct the group's attention to it at the start. Laminating this poster will also increase its durability.
3. List guidelines on a handout that can be distributed to the participants. You may want to incorporate this into a handout that includes fingerplays and other program-related material.

You can use the guidelines provided in Figures 4-1 and 4-2 in Appendix C (which may be reproduced) or creating your own. Here are some basic concepts to include:

1. Adults participate! Children take their cues from their parents/ caregivers. If the adults can relax and actively participate in the

program, the children will too. Remember this is a group experience that may be new to many of the children—and the adults, too.

2. Please put toys, food and other distractions away during the program. Bottles or other "not-to-be-parted-with" items are okay but should be used discreetly. This also applies to breastfeeding.

3. Start on time. The children are "fresh" when they arrive, so take advantage of it. If the room is reserved for sufficient time prior to and after the program there will be time for the participants to interact and share.

4. If a child seems overwhelmed, cries, or generally "loses it," adult caregivers should feel free to step outside and regroup, then return to the group or try again another time. Caregivers should talk with the presenter about any concern they may have about their child's behavior.

5. RELAX! The child's participation in all of the activities is not expected. The goal is to have fun with books, rhymes, songs, and other language-building play.

PART 2: THE STORY TIME

This part of the program consists of stories from books suitable for this age group, finger rhymes, and songs. It lasts approximately twenty to twenty-five minutes. Creating a fun-filled experience with language and literature for the participants as well as being a role model for reading aloud is a major purpose of this part of the program. Interaction between the presenter and the group can demonstrate how to read to a very young child and often encourage the adult to shed self-consciousness. Very young children will be inclined to want to share in the experience the joy of stories, rhymes, and songs.

It is important to be flexible with the materials actually used for this program, so it is best to have more material than you will actually need. You can vary the duration of the program by the number of finger rhymes, songs, and stories you use. This is useful when you have to adapt to the group dynamics. For example, an active group may need more action rhymes, whereas a more attentive group may prefer to hear the stories.

The general format of the story time is as follows:

1. opening song or rhyme
2. finger rhyme/action rhyme/bounce/song
3. story
4. finger rhyme/action rhyme/bounce/song
5. story
6. finger rhyme/action rhyme/bounce/song

7. story
8. finger rhyme/action rhyme/bounce/song
9. closing song or rhyme

By varying the number of finger rhymes, bounces, and songs, the program will change. There should always be one story read aloud, with the possibility of adding others. It is also possible to read the story more than once or repeat rhymes and songs. The children have favorites and love to do them again and again.

It may be tempting to increase the time for this part of the program, because it really is fun. Keep in mind the children are absorbing everything that is said and done in the class even when they may not be actively participating. But try not to compress too many literary experiences into the time frame, or overstimulation may be the result. Children need time to absorb and process what they are hearing and doing. A sense of wanting more of a wonderful program is a way to encourage the adults to recreate the literacy literature experience at home (Ernst, 1995: 37).

Basic program outlines have been written out in *Lapsit Services for the Very Young* (Ernst, 1995). More programs are outlined in this text, and additional resources for program ideas are listed at the end of this chapter.

PART 3: ADULT EDUCATION

The presenter may sometimes find this section a stumbling block. This program has wonderful entertainment value, but it is also a language-learning experience, and one of its major purposes is to create library users and promote literacy. It should also serve as an empowerment experience for the parent or caregiver.

Education can be approached in many ways and is best kept simple. Booktalking, displays, handouts, or even simple comments during the program as to the benefits and importance of rhymes, stories, and other activities are all education, as is letting the participants know about library services and materials they may be unaware of. One of the simplest means of education is to place a table by the exit. In addition to displaying books, place on it library flyers and applications, handouts, and other "for your information" materials so that they can be easily picked up. If you have a business card, make that available as well. You want the adults in the group to feel that they have a friendly contact at the library. Make it a point to mention the location of the library when doing this program as outreach and some of the other available services they could use for job searches and other personal needs.

PART 4: BONUS

This section relates to the time allowed for interaction and dialog among the participants. This may be the only activity for parents to participate in with their child and give them a chance to see their child interact with others the same age. Young mothers especially welcome the opportunity to visit one-to-one with other young women. Some ideas might be to bring out a collection of board books, blow bubbles while music plays, have some activity that the child and adult can do together, and thus give the adults a chance to share and talk. You can also encourage the adult participants to share a story or rhyme from their own family. The presenter should be available during this follow-up time to answer questions, give individual consultations, give a tour of the facility, supply resources, and talk individually with the adults. This time makes the parent/adult and the child feel welcome and helps create a positive experience.

THINGS TO CONSIDER

With the increasing popularity of programming for the pretoddler a few major concerns have developed. Each library is unique in its facility, staffing, and policies, so no one answer is absolute. A variety of options need to be created, of which only one may meet the need.

Crowd control has become a large concern. Often in striving to build a clientele, we are faced with the problem of what happens when there is no room for everyone who wants to attend. When crowd control becomes an issue, there are limits that need to be set. These limits are not arbitrary but important to ensure a fun and memorable learning/ literary experience for all who attend. This program is not just something to keep the little ones busy with for awhile.

Look first as to what limits you have in house. The size of the room will dictate the maximum number for safety reasons. The number of staff doing such programs will dictate how often this program can be offered. The space has to be filled with the number of participants that the presenter feels comfortable working with without losing command. These story times are always pretty lively, but you do not want utter chaos!

There are some possible solutions when the number of participants exceeds the space available:

1. Registration for the program may become necessary. Although this is time consuming, there are some benefits. It gives you a definite number of participants who will take part, which is useful when preparing materials for the program. You will also have a record after the fact of how many people were actually in the group and their names and addresses. You can create a waiting

list to help evaluate the impact of this program and decide on the number of times it is to be offered and when. People who register tend to commit themselves to attending the program on a regular basis. Having phone numbers is also useful if you want to do follow up or develop a connection with them.

2. Offer two classes back-to-back so that the same program material can be used with two different groups of participants. Two morning classes or even two early evening classes may be a possibility. If you try this, be sure to include in your publicity that both classes are identical and attendance at only one is allowed. A poster stating this at the program room's entrance will serve as a good reminder.

3. When the maximum number of participants has been reached, be firm. Post a sign saying the class is full and to please attend the next one or speak to the librarian/presenter. Hopefully you won't have to post a staff member at the door to enforce this rule.

4. Offer this class as a series for a limited number of weeks. In this case, you may want to register participants for the series to encourage consistency in attendance. A different group would then be allowed to sign up for the next series so you could serve more people.

5. Check with other libraries in your area. Perhaps you can cooperate and each offer the class once a month on a different day and at a different site. This cooperation is called a "Round Robin" at the King County Library System in Washington. Four libraries located within driving distance of each other offer a program called "Mother Goose on the Loose." Each library takes one week a month to offer a story time for the very young, and each library decides which day during their week works best for them. In this way, there is something each week for the very young child in the area.

6. You may find out that a portion of your participants is actually a group such as a playgroup or mother-support group. Setting up a program just for them may free up some room.

Too large a crowd can also occur because more than just the target audience is present—usually an older or younger child attending. Restricting the program to the particular age child and accompanying adult intended ensures one-on-one interaction of each pair with each other and the rest of the group without distractions. Publicity should reflect this by stating "One adult lap per child." The librarian/presenter is the one who can determine the flexibility of this rule. If an older sibling has to attend, remind the adult this program is aimed at the very young child and that is where your attention will be. Suggest that a doll or stuffed toy might be called upon to be the older sibling's "little one" during the program.

Another problem is latecomers. These can prove to be a distraction and disrupt the class. Since these programs tend to be brief (as few as twenty minutes), it creates problems when people walk in with only a few minutes left. It may be necessary to speak with chronic latecomers personally. Indicate first that it is great they are making the effort to attend but that some adjustments need to be made. Information about the starting time and approximate duration needs to be on your publicity, made into a sign, included in your guideline handouts, and even verbally expressed to the participants at the program.

Finally, many presenters have concerns regarding the adult participation in the program. The adults sometimes get so busy talking among themselves that they become a distraction to the group, especially the presenter. How does one mend this problem? The simplest way is to involve the adults directly with the literary experience and the child. Establish the "rule" that the children can watch but the adults must participate right up front to set the tone. Varying the volume and pitch of your voice sometimes can draw them back. For example, lowering the volume of your voice makes their voices more noticeable so they may become self-conscious and stop talking. Sudden changes or sounds works as well—for example, whistling like a bird or barking like the dog in Bill Martin's *Brown Bear, Brown Bear* has always caught their attention. If need be, remind the adults that there will be time after the program for talking. One of my favorite ways to get the adults back into the program is to ask the little ones if the big people are asleep. "They must be asleep," I say, "'cause I don't hear them joining in! Let's help them!" Another method is to have the child get the adult's attention: Ask the child to do a rhyme's action with the adult. For example, have the child touch the adult's head, shoulders, knees, and toes, or be the cobbler and tap on the adult's shoe. The more you actively engage both the child and the adult in the experience, the less chance there is for disruptive conversations to take place.

TIPS

Here are some suggestions to help your program be the best it can be.

1. Wear comfortable clothing. Now is not the time for fancy or form-fitting clothing, since there will be a lot of movement during the program. I have found that pants work very well, especially ones with pockets where you can hide finger puppets, a "cheat sheet" (an index card with a list of stories, rhymes, songs you plan to use), and a tissue (runny noses are often in attendance). Some people are more comfortable with a storytelling apron or smock, which can be used in the same capacity.

2. Limit jewelry and accessories. Children are attracted to things that are bright, shiny, and eye catching. They have a tendency to grab for the item, and you do not want to distract them from the program.

3. Use what you are comfortable with and have experience with. This is true for using puppets, picture cards, boomboxes, and any other props. Practice with them prior to the program.

4. Do not try to pack too many different presentations into one program. For example, using six to eight different puppets or many different CDs or tapes that need to be changed can be difficult and give the program a cluttered feeling. You want to create a smooth flow to your program with some variation in presentation, but not an elaborate production.

5. Select your books carefully. If you have a large group in attendance, a small board book will be difficult to share—even if it is a wonderful one; in this case, you may be able to supply enough copies of a small book for each adult/child pair to look at together while you read the story aloud. Remember also to select and order the books to suit the program: If it is an evening program a "quiet" story such as *Grandfather Twilight* by Barbara Berger or *I Hear* by Rachel Isadora would be better to close with than *If You Are Happy and You Know it Clap Your Hands* by David Carter.

6. Keep materials out of the children's reach and be aware of safety. Out of sight is often the best idea. Displaying the books you read is a nice idea, but often a book is picked up by a child who wants to share it with his adult. Limiting distraction in the presenter's area will help stop this from happening. Boomboxes with cords can be potential hazards for children to trip over or play with, so place the boomboxes in a location that will prevent this. Be aware of open electrical outlets, curtain cords, and the like that may present dangers.

7. Examine the program room before the program. A quick check of the floor for sharp objects, stacks of chairs that could be climbed on or tipped over, and open electrical outlets that need to be covered can be taken care of at that time. Remind adults prior to beginning the program that they are ultimately responsible for keeping their child safe while in the room.

8. Read expressively and use facial expressions. Varying the pitch and volume of your voice is a great way to gain the group's attention and even help regulate it. Children this age get many of their cues from body language, so be aware of what you are doing.

9. Use a "cheat sheet." It is absolutely all right to have an index card or small sheet of paper with the stories, songs, rhymes, and

activities you intend to use written on it close by; I keep mine in my pocket! It will often help you to stay focused, because this group can get really involved in the story-time program.

10. Do not be afraid to change words, make up your own tune, or in general make a mistake. First of all, the program participants will probably not even notice. Second, it is a perfect example of how they can do things like make up their own tunes or rhymes. By relaxing and making light of a mistake, you give the adults permission to not do everything perfectly correct all the time.

11. Keep your program simple. If you are introducing new material, explain it before involving the group and demonstrating it. Do not assume that everyone knows the rhyme or song, for example. You may want to create a poster with the words for display during the program, use a large pad that sits on a table or easel with the words on it, put new material together on a handout, or simply do the new piece a number of times throughout the program.

12. Do not be afraid to repeat the material more than once. A favorite rhyme the children love is always fun to do. Ask the adult participants if they would like to share a favorite family rhyme with the group or one they remember from their own childhood.

13. Give the program a framework. Use the same song to open and close your program such as clapping and singing "The More We Get Together" or use the same rhyme, for instance, "Patty Cake, Patty Cake," which most people know or at least can clap along with.

14. Respect the child. Keep the pace of the program moving, but do not rush it. Children can only process and absorb what they hear at a certain pace. Let the children know what you are going to do next. For instance, I will ask the children, "Would you like to hear a story?" or tell them "I'm going to read/tell you a story now" before I pick up the book. Besides moving them to the story portion of the program, it also prepares them to anticipate the wonderful experience to come. Eye contact also helps the presenter connect with the child and adult. The main point is to include the child and adult actively in the program.

TO THEME OR NOT TO THEME

Librarians' programs are as variedly creative as the librarians themselves. The major difference in many cases is that some librarians use a thematic approach, while others do not. Some feel that themes are necessary in order to create a program that flows evenly, plus a theme helps in selecting materials. Other librarians insist that themes are unnecessary and prefer to create more of a potpourri of activities for their programs. The age group we are working with, the 12-to-24-month-old child, in reality does not need a new theme with every program. Repeating selected program pieces will help establish a routine and a familiarity for the child. This is not to say themes should not be used. Adults often are able to remember more if a theme is evident and may wish to continue the literary experience outside the program itself. Themes will often give order to a program and ease in selection of materials. So to theme or not to theme? Either way works. It is up to the presenter as to which is more comfortable and which goes over best. In general, you can plan a core, consistently used program pattern consisting of an opening and closing with one story and rhymes/songs. You can then create a thematic program by adding your selected theme stories, rhymes, and songs if that is your style. The entire program does not need to be brand new every time. Remember this age group is comfortable with the familiar routine.

ANNOTATED BIBLIOGRAPHY

The following is a bibliography of more than 100 titles that have been successfully used by librarians with this lapsit age group. They are arranged alphabetically by author, list bibliographic material, give a brief summary and notes of interest, and conclude with suggested themes the book can be used for. The next section contains a subject index that groups these titles by theme.

Theme or no theme, utilize these books in the manner that serves you and your program best.

Apperley, Dawn. *Animal Moves*. New York: Little, Brown, 1989.
Animals make all kinds of movements, and by pulling tabs and lifting flaps these sturdy pages bring them to life. Children can be encouraged to move like the animals do. One animal per two-page spread. Tabs and flaps are easy to manipulate. (Animals, Movable Books, Movement, Participation)

——. *Animal Noises*. New York: Little, Brown, 1998.
Animals make all kinds of sounds, and by pulling tabs and lifting flaps these sturdy pages encourage the children to make animal sounds too. Double-spread pages illustrate only one animal at a time, which keeps it simple. Tabs and flaps are easy to manipulate. (Animals, Movable Books, Movement, Participation, Sounds)

Arnosky, Jim. *Come Out, Muskrats*. New York: Lothrop, Lee, and Shepard, 1989.
Muskrats play in their pond late in the afternoon. Illustrations work well with text. (Animals, Water)

Asch, Frank. *Baby in the Box*. New York: Holiday House, 1989.
Baby, fox, and ox have lots of fun with blocks and a box. (Babies, Play, Rhyming Story)

————. *Just Like Daddy*. New York: Simon & Schuster, 1981.
Going fishing with Daddy is a lot of fun, especially because Little Bear can do things "just like Daddy." Good to share with a group, since most scenes are a two-page spread. (Bears, Families, Fathers)

Axworthy, Ann. *Along Came Toto*. Cambridge, Mass.: Candlewick, 1993.
Percy the dog does not like Toto the kitten, who follows him everywhere. He discovers sometimes it is good to have a buddy around. The phrase "Along came Toto" is easy for everyone to join in on during the telling. (Cats, Dogs, Friends)

Baker, Keith. *Big Fat Hen*. New York: Harcourt Brace, 1994.
The familiar counting rhyme is accompanied by large, beautiful pictures for group sharing. (Chickens, Counting/Numbers, Rhyming Story)

Bang, Molly. *Ten, Nine, Eight*. New York: Mulberry, 1991.
Ending the day becomes a quiet countdown to bedtime. (Bedtime, Counting/Numbers, Rhyming Story)

Beck, Ian. *Five Little Ducks*. New York: Henry Holt, 1993.
This traditional counting rhyme is perfectly illustrated for all to share in the ducklings' adventure away from mother. Illustrations work well with groups. (Adventure, Counting/Numbers, Ducks, Exploring, Rhyming Story, Songs)

Berger, Barbara. *Grandfather Twilight*. New York: Philomel, 1984.
Grandfather Twilight takes his walk as nighttime approaches. A different and beautiful variation of a bedtime story, with delightful artwork. (Bedtime)

Berry, Holly. *Busy Lizzie*. New York: North-South, 1994.
Busy Lizzie is busy throughout the whole day clapping hands, rubbing her belly, and finding other fun ways to identify body parts. (Bedtime, Body Awareness, Movement, Participation, Play)

Bornstein, Ruth. *Little Gorilla*. New York: Clarion, 1976.
All the animals in the jungle love Little Gorilla, even when he gets bigger. (Animals, Animals—Jungle, Birthdays, Growing Up, Size)

Boynton, Sandra. *Good Night, Good Night*. New York: Random House, 1985.
All the animals on board a boat get ready for bed. Clear cartoon illustrations with rhyming text. (Animals, Bedtime, Rhyming Story)

Brown, Craig. *My Barn*. New York: Greenwillow, 1991.
The farmer listens to the sounds of the animals that live in his barn. (Animals, Animals—Farm, Farms, Sounds)

Brown, Marc. *Marc Brown's Favorite Hand Rhymes*. New York: Dutton, 1999.
This book has nice illustrations of hand rhymes and has visual directions on movements next to each line. (Participation, Poetry)

Brown, Margaret Wise. *The Golden Egg Book*. New York: Golden Press, 1947.
A little bunny is all alone when he finds an egg. After trying to open it, he falls asleep, only to awaken and find a friend. (Animals, Ducks, Rabbits)

————. *Goodnight Moon*. New York: HarperCollins' Children's Books, 1947.
The classic story of a little one having to say goodnight to everyone and everything before he closes his eyes. (Bedtime, Rabbits, Rhyming Story)

————. *Home for a Bunny*. Racine, Wisc.: Golden Press, c1956.
Bunny needs to find a home, but every place he looks is already taken. (Rabbits)

Browne, Anthony. *I Like Books*. New York: Dragonfly, 1988.
A small chimp tells about all the different kinds of books he likes. (Concepts, Rhyming Story)

Burns, Kate. *Blink Like an Owl*. London: Levinson Children's Books, 1997.
The text involves the children by asking questions such as "Can you roar like a tiger?" when lifting the flap. Bold colors are outlined in white. (Animals, Movable Books, Movement, Participation)

————. *Waddle Like a Duck!* London: Levinson Children's Books, 1997.

The text involves the children by asking if they can do the same action the animal depicted is doing. Lift-the-flap book with sturdy pages. (Animals, Movable Books, Movement, Participation)

Burton, Marilee Robin. *Tail Toes Eyes Ears Nose.* New York: HarperCollins' Children's Books, 1992.
Parts of an animal are drawn on one page. The reader has to guess which animal it really is. Possible use as picture-card story or flannel board. Eight animals depicted in all. (Animals, Games, Response Books)

Butterworth, Nick. *Just Like Jasper!* Boston: Little, Brown, 1989.
Jasper goes to the store to buy a special toy. Pages are a nice size for sharing with groups. and text is simple. Illustrations are clear and brightly colored. (Cats, Toys)

Cabrera, Jane. *Panda Big and Panda Small.* New York: DK Publishers, 1998.
Panda Big and Panda Small find the many ways they are different, but agree they like being together best of all. (Bears, Concepts, Rhyming Story, Size)

Carle, Eric. *From Head to Toe.* New York: HarperCollins' Children's Books, 1997.
Children see if they can mimic the actions of animals. (Animals, Exercise, Movement, Participation)

————. *Little Cloud.* New York: Philomel, 1996.
In a bright blue sky, a little white cloud tries out different shapes till it decides to join the rest of the clouds and rain. (Clouds, Rain, Shapes, Weather)

————. *What's for Lunch?* New York: Putnam, 1998.
Monkey swings through the trees looking for his lunch. (Counting/Numbers, Food, Monkeys, Movable Books)

Carlson, Nancy. *I Like Me!* New York: Viking Kestrel, 1998,
With positive thinking and a good self-image, this pig proves you can be your own best friend and have fun on your own. (Friends, Pigs)

Carroll, Kathleen Sullivan. *One Red Rooster.* Boston: Houghton Mifflin, 1992.
This rhyming text counts the animals on the farm, one to ten. Art work is bold in color and stylized for clarity. (Animals, Animals—Farm, Counting/Numbers, Farms, Rhyming Story)

Carter, David. *If You're Happy and You Know It, Clap Your Hands: A Pop-Up Book.* New York: Scholastic, 1997.
This is a wonderful book to sing along with. Tabs are easy to manipulate on sturdy pages. (Response Books, Rhyming Story, Songs)

————. *Says Who?* New York: Simon & Schuster, 1993.
A pop-up book of animal sounds. (Animals, Games, Movable Books, Response Books, Sounds)

Cauley, Lorinda Bryan. *Clap Your Hands.* New York: Putnam, 1992.
Find rhymes here to act out: clap your hands, roar like a lion, and other fun activities. (Movement, Participation, Play, Rhyming Story)

Chorao, Kay. *Knock at the Door and Other Baby Action Rhymes.* New York: Dutton, 1999.
Beautiful illustrations of twenty action rhymes with the directions for movements next to the line in a small box. The directions are illustrated using simple line drawings, clear enough to understand without words. This book can be used to present rhymes visually or as a resource book for finger rhymes. (Participation, Poetry)

Cimarusti, Marie. *Peek a Moo!* New York: Dutton, 1998.
Combining flap pages and animal sounds, this fun book has everyone joining in the game of peek-a-boo. (Animals, Animals—Farm, Games, Movable Books, Sounds)

Cony, Frances. *Old MacDonald Had a Farm.* New York: Orchard, 1999.
This movable book of tabs, flaps, and dials shows the animals singing along with the reader. Pages are sturdy and fairly easy to manipulate. (Animals, Animals—Farms, Farms, Movable Book, Songs)

Cousins, Lucy. *What Can Rabbit See?* New York: Tambourine, 1991.
With his new glasses, rabbit can see lots of things; by lifting the flaps, so can the reader. Pages are sturdy and easy to use. (Movable Books, Rabbits, Senses)

Crews, Donald. *Freight Train.* New York: Greenwillow, 1978.
Bright colors and brief text name the parts of a freight train as it moves along its journey. (Colors, Things That Go, Trains)

Dabcovich, Lydia. *Ducks Fly.* New York: Dutton, 1990.
A little duck has trouble learning to fly like his brothers and sisters. Brief text with double-spread illustrations in wonderful colors. (Animals, Ducks)

—————. *Sleepy Bear*. New York: Dutton, 1982.
Bear falls asleep in the fall only to be awakened in the spring when the bees arrive to make honey. Artwork and text are perfect for this age group. (Bears, Seasons)

Demarest, Chris L. *Honk!* Honesdale, Penna.: Boyds Mills Press, 1998.
Searching for her mother, Little Goose hears all the other animals reply to her question with their own sound. (Animals, Animals—Farms, Families, Farms, Mothers, Movable Books, Sounds)

—————. *My Blue Boat*. San Diego: Harcourt, 1995.
A little girl imagines her toy boat sails further than the confines of the bathtub. (Bathtime, Boats, Imagination, Things That Go, Water)

Deming, A. G. *Who Is Tapping at My Window?* New York: Dutton, 1988.
A little girl asks the animals if they are the ones tapping at her window. Finally the raindrops answer. (Rain, Rhyming Story, Weather)

Dijs, Carla. *Are You My Daddy?* New York: Little, Simon, 1990.
Little Tiger cannot find his daddy, so he asks all the other animals if they are his daddy. (Animals, Animals—Jungle, Families, Fathers, Movable Books, Response Books)

—————. *Are You My Mommy?* New York: Little, Simon, 1990.
Searching for his mother, Little Chick meets many animals and asks his question. (Animals, Families, Mothers, Movable Books, Response Books)

Duffy, Dee Dee. *Barnyard Tracks*. Honesdale, Penna.: Bell Books, 1992.
Bright primary colors illustrate different farm animals' tracks. Hints are given on pages, and the animal's sound is on the same page as its tracks are illustrated in black. Following these pages is a double-page spread with the answers in full color. Brief story of fox's tracks appearing and farmer chasing it away. Large pages, good for groups. (Animals—Farm, Farms, Response Books)

Elgar, Rebecca. *Is That an Elephant Over There?* London: Levinson Children's Books, 1995.
A simple question is asked, and lifting the flap gives the animal answer. Children enjoy saying "NO" until finally the elephant appears. Board-book format but size is okay for group viewing. (Animals, Animals—Jungle, Elephants, Games, Movable Books, Response Books)

Evans, Katie. *Hunky Dory Ate It!* New York: Puffin Unicorn, 1992. Hunky Dory eats everything and ends up with a tummy ache. (Dogs, Food, Rhyming Story)

————. *Hunky Dory Found It!* New York: Dutton, 1994. Hunky Dory loves to find things and keep them for himself. (Dogs, Games, Rhyming Story)

Flack, Marjorie. *Ask Mr. Bear*. New York: Macmillan, 1932. Danny asks the animals to help him give his mother a gift. Mr. Bear has the perfect answer. This can be made into a flannel-board story or used with puppets. It is also fun to have the children give the adult they are with a hug at the conclusion. (Animals, Bears, Birthdays, Mothers)

Fleming, Denise. *Barnyard Banter*. New York: Henry Holt, 1994. Looking and listening to the animals on the farm, goose is hiding on every page. Wonderful, brilliantly colored illustrations. (Animals, Animals—Farms, Farms, Response Book, Rhyming Story, Sounds)

————. *In the Small, Small Pond*. New York: Henry Holt, 1993. A frog's-eye view of how the seasons change the pond where it lives. (Animals, Outside, Rhyming Story, Seasons, Water)

————. *In the Tall, Tall Grass*. New York: Henry Holt, 1991. The rhyming text gives a bug's-eye view of what one may find in the grass when exploring. (Adventure, Animals, Bugs, Outside, Rhyming Stories)

————. *Lunch*. New York: Henry Holt, 1992. Mouse is hungry and makes a mess while eating his lunch. Large pages with brilliantly colored illustrations. (Colors, Food, Manners, Messes, Mice)

————. *Mama Cat Has Three Kittens*. New York: Henry Holt, 1998. Kittens learn from their mama, but little Boris has his own way of learning. (Babies, Cats, Mothers)

Ford, Miela, and Tana Hoban. *Little Elephant*. New York: Greenwillow, 1994. Exploring the water, Little Elephant has a wonderful adventure. (Adventure, Animals—Jungle, Elephants, Water)

Fox, Mem. *Time for Bed*. New York: Harcourt, 1993. The animal parents get their children ready to go to bed. (Bedtime, Families, Rhyming Story)

French, Vivian, and Alex Ayliffe. *Oh No, Anna!* Atlanta: Peachtree, 1997.
Anna creates different-colored messes while her mother is busy elsewhere. Lift-the-flap pages. (Colors, Exploring, Messes, Participation)

Gag, Wanda. *The ABC Bunny*. New York: Coward-McCann, 1933.
An alphabet rhyming story that has been around a long time. Easy story to memorize, as bunny explores the world around him one fine day. (Animals, Rabbits, Rhyming Story)

Gillham, Bill. *And So Can I!* New York: Putnam, 1987.
This story has the child copy the movements of various animals. Uses photographs, but size is best used for small groups. (Animals, Movement, Participation)

Ginsburg, Mirra. *Across the Stream*. New York: Greenwillow, 1982.
A bad dream chases Mother Hen and her chicks. Rescued by Mother Duck and her ducklings, the bad dream has a happy ending. Illustrations are bold colors and the text is brief. (Adventure, Animals, Chickens, Ducks, Water)

————. *Asleep, Asleep*. New York: Greenwillow, 1992.
It's time to sleep as baby is put to bed by Mother. Quiet, rich story with simple text. (Animals, Bedtime)

————. *Good Morning, Chick*. New York: Greenwillow, 1980.
Simple story of a newborn chick's first day on the farm. Has repeating line—"just like this"—that brings attention back to the story. Illustrations are bright and clear. (Animals—Farm, Chickens, Farms)

Hale, Sarah Josepha. *Mary Had a Little Lamb*. New York: Scholastic, 1990.
Bruce McMillan has updated this familiar rhyming story of Mary's little lamb. This photo-illustrated version is in a contemporary setting and uses children of many cultures to tell the story. (Poetry, Rhyming Story, Sheep, Songs)

Halpern, Shari. *Little Robin Redbreast: A Mother Goose Rhyme*. New York: North-South Books, 1994.
A little robin outwits a cat. Pages are big with artwork created from cut-paper collage, using paper painted with acrylics. (Birds, Cats, Poetry, Rhyming Story)

Henderson, Kathy. *Bounce, Bounce, Bounce*. Cambridge, Mass.: Candlewick Press, 1994.

A rhyming story that demonstrates how things are used from the viewpoint of a toddler. For example, chairs are for bouncing, saucepans for crashing. (Play, Rhyming Story)

Hill, Eric. *Where's Spot?* New York: Putnam, 1980.
The first of the Spot "lift-the-flap" books. Simple story of looking for puppy Spot who has missed his dinner. Children love to give the answer "NO!" after each flap is lifted. (Dogs, Movable Books, Response Story)

Hubbel, Patricia. *Pots and Pans*. New York: HarperCollins' Children's Books, 1998.
Great story of how baby gets into the pots and pans, creating a glorious concert of sound. Size of book allows for group viewing, and rhyming text is fun to read aloud. (Babies, Games, Messes, Play, Sounds)

Hughes, Shirley. *Bathwater's Hot*. New York: Lothrop, Lee and Shepard, 1985.
This rhyming story tells how a little girl discovers that the things she sees have opposites. (Concepts, Rhyming Story)

————. *Bouncing*. Cambridge, Mass.: Candlewick Press, 1993.
Bouncing can be done all kinds of different ways, and a little girl explores lots of them. (Movement, Play)

————. *Giving*. Cambridge, Mass.: Candlewick Press, 1993.
A little girl and her brother discover you can give all different kinds of things, some of which make you happy, others not. (Giving/Sharing)

Hutchins, Pat. *Titch*. New York: Macmillan, 1971.
Titch may be little, but he certainly shows his big brother and sister that being little is special, too. (Families, Gardens, Toys)

Isadora, Rachel. *I Hear*. New York: Greenwillow, 1985.
Story follows the sounds a child might hear from the time of waking until falling asleep. Although small in size (7"x8"), pictures share two-page spreads. (Bedtime, Senses, Sounds)

————. *I See*. New York: Greenwillow, 1985.
A book that is fun to read to little ones who are starting to notice the world around them and name what they see. (Babies, Senses)

Jaynes, Ruth. *Benny's Four Hats*. Glendale, Calif.: Bowman, 1967.
Photo story of Benny's day when he puts on a certain hat. Simple

question of wondering why involves the listeners. (Hats, Response Books, Weather)

Jonas, Ann. *Now We Can Go*. New York: Greenwillow, 1986.
Child must decide what to take along on an outing. One page has everything in a box, with the bag open on the facing page. Story can also be acted out, with actual items moved from a box to bag. It would also work as a flannel-board story. (Toys)

————. *When You Were a Baby*. New York: Greenwillow, 1982.
Child is reminded of all the things he or she could not do as a baby. (Babies, Growing Up)

Kalan, Robert. *Blue Sea*. New York: Greenwillow, 1972.
Little fish, big fish, bigger fish, and biggest fish meet up in the blue sea. (Concepts, Fish, Size, Water)

————. *Rain*. New York: Greenwillow, 1978.
A rainstorm is described with brief text and illustrations in bold colors. (Colors, Rain, Weather)

Kraus, Robert. *Whose Mouse Are You?* New York: Macmillan, 1970.
Aruego's bold illustrations bring this simple story to life. In response to the question, the little mouse connects with his family and has an adventure on the way. (Adventure, Babies, Families, Mice)

Krauss, Ruth. *Bears*. New York: Harper Collins' Children's Books, 1948.
A rhyming story that finds bears everywhere. Has been available in big-book format as well. (Bears, Rhyming Story)

————. *The Carrot Seed*. New York: HarperCollins' Children's Books, 1945.
A little boy plants a carrot seed that no one thinks will grow. Available in a big-book format, can be done as a flannel-board story or with props. (Gardens)

Langstaff, John. *Oh, A-Hunting We Will Go*. New York: Atheneum, 1974.
This is a fun story to sing along with. Can be modified as to length and animals "caught." Works well as a flannel-board story also. (Animals, Rhyming Story, Song)

————. *Over in the Meadow*. New York: Harcourt, 1957.
Lovely illustrations accompany the familiar counting song of childhood. (Animals, Counting/Numbers, Rhyming Story, Songs)

Lawrence, Michael. *Baby Loves*. New York: DK Publishing, 1999.
Find out what baby loves best in this fun romp through baby's day.
Fun pictures for all; even adults will laugh at what baby is actually
illustrated doing. (Babies, Daily Life, Families)

Lawston, Lisa. *Can You Hop?* New York: Orchard, 1999.
Froggy wants to go hopping with a friend, but who else among the
animals hops? Fun search with a "hoppy" ending. Board book. (Animals, Participation)

Lear, Edward. *The Owl and the Pussycat*. New York: Putnam, 1991.
Jan Brett has created wonderfully detailed illustrations of Lear's story
poem. Set in the Caribbean, and brilliant colors fill the pages. Story
is easy to memorize. (Animals, Birds, Cats, Poetry, Rhyming Story)

————. *The Owl and the Pussycat*. New York: Clarion, 1987.
Paul Galdone's cartoon illustrations help tell the story of Lear's poem.
Pages are big enough to share with a large group. (Animals, Birds,
Cats, Poetry, Rhyming Story)

Lewis, Kevin. *Chugga-Chugga Choo-Choo*. New York: Hyperion,
1999.
A freight train's day from dawn 'til night, all from the viewpoint of
a toy train. (Rhyming Story, Things That Go, Toys, Trains)

Lillie, Patricia. *Everything Has a Place*. New York: Greenwillow, 1993.
Large colorful pictures help a little child learn that everything has a
place—from a bird in a nest to a book on a shelf. (Daily Life)

Maris, Ron. *In My Garden*. New York: Greenwillow, 1987.
Looking at her garden, a girl sees all the animals and friends she
has. Story is told using half pages that hide and then reveal the illustrations. (Gardens)

————. *Runaway Rabbit*. New York: Greenwillow, 1989.
A pet rabbit meets animals as he runs away from his master. Uses
half page or split page to move the story along. (Adventure, Animals, Rabbits)

Martin, Bill. *Brown Bear, Brown Bear, What Do You See?* New York:
Henry Holt, 1967.
A popular title for this age group, this question/answer rhyming
story uses bold artwork and encourages the listeners to join the story
telling. (Animals, Colors, Participation, Response Books, Rhyming
Story)

————. *Here Are My Hands.* New York: Henry Holt, 1985.
Discover parts of the body with a simple text in rhyme. (Body Awareness, Rhyming Story)

McDonnell, Flora. *I Love Animals.* Cambridge, Mass.: Candlewick Press, 1994.
All the animals on the farm are loved by a child, who identifies each one. Illustrations are perfect size to share with a group. (Animals, Animals—Farms, Farms)

————. *I Love Boats.* Cambridge, Mass.: Candlewick Press, 1995.
A little girl names all the different boats she loves to watch and sail in her bathtub. Big illustrations are wonderful to share. (Bathtime, Boats, Things That Go, Water)

————. *Splash!* Cambridge, Mass.: Candlewick Press, 1999.
Baby elephant comes up with a great idea to cool off all the animals on a really hot day. Large-sized pages are good for group sharing. (Elephants, Animals—Jungle, Water)

Miller, Margaret. *Whose Hat?* New York: Greenwillow, 1988.
Photos of hats with the question "Whose hat?" are answered with clear-colored photos of adult employed in that occupation and a child actually wearing the hat. (Hats, Occupations)

Morgan, Mary. *Gentle Rosie.* New York: Hyperion, 1999.
Small book tells story of Rosie's day and the things the little mouse does. (Mice)

Newcome, Zita. *Toddlerobics.* Cambridge, Mass.: Candlewick Press, 1996.
Wonderful rhyming story of a group of toddlers doing their exercises. Fun to have children not only listen to the story but also act it out. (Body Awareness, Exercise, Movement, Participation, Rhyming Story)

————. *Toddlerobics Animal Fun.* Cambridge, Mass.: Candlewick Press, 1999.
A lively group of toddlers discover lots of fun when they move like the different animals do. (Animals, Exercise, Movement, Participation, Rhyming Story)

Offen, Hilda. *A Fox Got My Socks.* New York: Dutton, 1992.
Getting dressed was never so much fun as when animals try on your clothes, too. (Getting Dressed, Participation, Rhyming Story)

————. *As Quiet as a Mouse.* New York: Dutton, 1994.
A fun and lively action-rhyme story gets the children acting out the animal actions described and making their sounds also. Pictures are bright and clear, pages about 7"x 9". (Animals, Movement, Participation, Rhyming Story)

Omerod, Jan. *The Saucepan Game.* New York: Lothrop, Lee and Shepard, 1989.
One kitten + one baby + one saucepan = lots of fun. Simple text moves the story along as all the possibilities of the saucepan are examined. You could use an actual pot and cover to tell the story. (Babies, Cats, Games, Imagination, Play)

Oxenbury, Helen. *Clap Hands.* New York: Aladdin, 1987.
This oversized board book with rhyming text illustrates multicultural children with large pictures and bright colors. (Babies, Sounds)

————. *Tickle, Tickle.* New York: Aladdin, 1987.
Illustrations of multicultural children are large and clear in bright colors. Oversized board book with rhyming lines. (Babies, Games, Sounds)

————. *Tom and Pippo Take a Walk.* New York: Aladdin, 1988.
Tom takes his toy monkey Pippo for a walk, gets muddy, and has to take a bath. (Bathtime, Monkeys, Outside, Toys)

————. *Tom and Pippo in the Snow.* New York: Aladdin, 1989.
Tom and Pippo have fun in the snow with Daddy. (Monkeys, Outside, Seasons, Toys)

Paul, Ann Whiteford. *Hello Toes! Hello Feet!* New York: DK Publishing, 1998.
A little girl has fun all day long following where her feet lead her. (Adventure, Body Awareness, Rhyming Stories)

Petersham, Maud and Miska. *The Box with Red Wheels.* New York: Macmillan, 1949.
In this gentle story, farm animals wonder what or who is in the box with red wheels. Beautiful illustrations framed in eye-catching red and yellow. Nice size pages for sharing with group. (Animals, Animals—Farm, Babies)

Pienkowski, J. *Trucks and Other Working Wheels.* New York: Dutton, 1997.
With bold, three-dimensional drawings, this pop-up book looks at

all kinds of working trucks. (Movable Books, Things That Go)

Pirotta, Saviour. *Little Bird*. New York: Tambourine, 1992.
Little Bird is at a loss as to what to do one day, so he asks all the animals he meets. Children can try to act out some of the suggestions he receives. Art work is bold and eye catching. (Animals, Birds, Movement, Participation)

Polushkin, Marie. *Who Said Meow?* New York: Bradbury, 1988.
Puppy investigates to find out who is making the new and unusual sound he hears. (Animals, Cats, Dogs, Sounds)

Pragoff, Fiona. *Where Is Alice's Bear?* New York: Bantam Doubleday Dell, 1999.
This pop-up book uses actual photographs of Alice as she looks for her bear and finds who is really hiding in the various places she looks. (Bears, Games, Movable Books)

Price, Matthew, and Jean Claver. *Peek-a-Boo*. New York: Knopf, 1985.
Asked who it might be hiding, the ensuing two-page spread opens to reveal the answer with a "peek-a-boo." Easy to manipulate. (Games, Movable Books, Response Book)

Raffi. *Five Little Ducks*. New York: Crown, 1989.
Mother Duck sets off to find her little ducklings after they disappear one by one. (Counting/Numbers, Ducks, Exploring, Songs)

Rice, Eve. *Benny Bakes a Cake*. New York: Greenwillow, 1981.
Benny's birthday cake is the center of this story—first the making of it, and then when his dog eats it. All is resolved in the end. Simple story line. (Birthdays, Dogs)

————. *Sam Who Never Forgets*. New York: Greenwillow, 1977.
Sam the zookeeper feeds all the zoo animals one day, but did he forget elephant? Artwork will appeal to this age group. (Animals, Elephants, Food, Occupations)

Roffey, Maureen. *Look, There's My Hat!* New York: Putnam, 1984.
A little girl thinks everyone else's hat, coat, shoes, and other pieces of attire are hers. Illustrations depict how these items really fit her. (Getting Dressed, Hats, Size)

Scott, Ann Herbert. *On Mother's Lap*. New York: Clarion, 1992.
Mother's lap can hold everything a little Eskimo boy would want,

but he is not sure there's room for baby. Simple text with a soothing repeating line that invites the participants to rock back and forth along with the child. (Babies, Families, Mothers)

Seuss, Dr. *My Many Colored Days*. New York: Knopf, 1996.
Rhyming story that uses colors to describe a day by associating its mood or feeling with a color. (Colors, Emotions, Rhyming Story)

Shaw, Nancy. *Sheep in a Jeep*. Boston: Houghton Mifflin, 1986.
A funny, rollicking, rhyming story of sheep driving a Jeep. Word sounds are great for reading aloud. (Rhyming Story, Sheep, Things That Go)

Shone, Venice. *Cock-a-Doodle-Doo! A Day on the Farm*. New York: Scholastic, 1991.
Animals enjoy the day on the farm from sunrise until night. Text uses short sentences and makes a good read aloud. (Animals—Farm, Farms)

Simmons, Jane. *Come Along Daisy!* New York: Little, Brown, 1997.
Duckling Daisy gets so involved in discovering her surroundings that she momentarily loses her mother. Artwork has bright colors, and page size makes this large enough to share with group. Story can be shortened as desired by turning from page where Daisy discovers herself alone to page where she hears rustling on the riverbank. The recurring line "Come along Daisy!" often is repeated by participants. (Ducks, Exploring, Mothers)

Stoeke, Janet Morgan. *Hide and Seek*. New York: Dutton, 1999.
Board book of adorable hen Minerva Louise. She doesn't see the animals hiding, but everyone looking will. Small size but bright, clear illustrations. (Animals, Animals—Farm, Birds, Chickens, Farms, Games, Play)

————. *Rainy Day*. New York: Dutton, 1999.
Another board book of the adorable hen Minerva Louise. When it starts to rain, how can she stay dry? What will she do if she gets wet? Small size but bright, clear illustrations. (Animals, Animals—Farm, Birds, Chickens, Farms, Games, Play)

Suteyev, V. *The Chick and the Duckling*. New York: Macmillan, 1972.
Chick wants to do everything duckling does, with some interesting results. (Adventure, Animals, Chickens, Ducks)

Tafuri, Nancy. *The Ball Bounced*. New York: Greenwillow, 1989.

With no more than three words per page, Tafuri has written a story that intrigues the listener. A ball goes bouncing through the house, and where will it go next? Bright art outlined in black adds clarity. (Movement, Toys)

————. *Have You Seen My Duckling?* New York: Greenwillow, 1984.
While mother duck is looking for her little one, he is off exploring the world. Children will enjoy spotting him in the illustrations while mother duck is looking elsewhere. (Ducks, Exploring, Mothers, Water)

————. *This Is the Farmer.* New York: Greenwillow, 1994.
A chain of events that begins with a farmer's kiss proves to be a lively romp. Children will enjoy looking for the mouse found on most pages. (Animals, Animals—Farm, Farms, Mice)

Twinem, Neecy. *Bug Hunt.* New York: Grosset and Dunlap, 1999.
Look and see what bugs are hiding in the great outdoors. Sturdy pages and flaps with easy-to-identify bugs. (Adventure, Bugs, Movable Books, Outside, Response Book)

Van Laan, Nancy. *Big Fat Worm.* New York: Random House, 1995.
A big fat worm meets a big fat bird, who in turn meets a big fat cat who meets a big fat dog. This circular tale has bright pictures and repeating phrases. To shorten this story, end when the dog chews his bone. (Animals, Birds, Bugs, Cats, Dogs)

Van Rynbach, Iris. *The Five Little Pumpkins.* Honesdale, Penna.: Boyds Mills, 1995.
The traditional finger rhyme is illustrated with large, easy-to-see illustrations. (Holidays, Rhyming Story, Seasons)

Walsh, Melanie. *Do Pigs Have Stripes?* Boston: Houghton Mifflin, 1996.
Animal identification story. Silly questions like, "Does a bird have a big, black, wet nose?" Correct answers given on next page. Presenter can adjust "length" of book by selecting some or all of the animals. (Animals, Pigs, Response Books)

Wantanabe, Shigeo. *How Do I Put It On?* New York: Philomel, 1977.
Getting dressed was never so fun as watching little bear do it himself. Book is on the small size (8" x 8"), but illustrations are very clear. Presenter may also use a stuffed toy and actually dress it while telling the story. (Bears, Getting Dressed)

Watson, Clyde. *Catch Me and Kiss Me and Say It Again.* New York: Philomel, 1978.
Book of poems that can be read individually and made into action rhymes for the children to act out. (Poetry)

Wells, Rosemary. *Noisy Nora.* New York: Dial, 1973.
In a new, larger format, Nora's actions to get attention can be shared with larger groups. This story has a rhyming text and the artwork is wonderful. (Families, Mice, Rhyming Story, Sounds)

Williams, Sue. *I Went Walking.* San Diego: Harcourt, 1989.
Out for a walk, a boy identifies the differently colored animals that he sees. (Adventure, Animals, Animals—Farms, Outside, Response Books, Rhyming Story)

————. *Let's Go Visiting.* San Diego: Harcourt, 1998.
Off on a day of visiting the animals on the farm, a child counts and gives the color of each one he sees. Available in big-book format and can also be told as a flannel-board story. (Animals, Animals—Farm, Counting/Numbers, Response Books, Rhyming Story)

Williams, Vera. *"More, More, More," Said the Baby.* New York: Greenwillow, 1990.
Father, Grandmother, and Mother each give their baby some loving attention. Three stories and each can be used on its own. (Babies, Families)

Wood, Don and Audrey. *The Little Mouse, the Red Ripe Strawberry, and the Big Hungry Bear.* New York: Child's Play (International), 1984.
The narrator/reader tells Little Mouse that the big hungry bear will find the strawberry no matter what. Artwork is clear, bright, colorful, and large enough for groups to see. All ages will delight in Little Mouse's ideas for hiding the berry—this is a good story to illustrate that picture books can be fun for adults, too. (Bears, Food, Mice)

————. *Piggies.* New York: Harcourt, 1991.
A rollicking tale is told as piggies dance across a child's fingertips. (Bedtime, Body Awareness, Games, Participation, Pigs)

Wood, Jakki. *Dads Are Such Fun.* New York: Simon and Schuster, 1992.
Little animals and human children find out that dads are fun. (Animals, Animals—Jungle, Families, Fathers)

THEME INDEX FOR BOOKS

In order to simplify planning and to save the presenter time, the books from the previous bibliography have been organized into themes or subjects. These are by no means the only titles available for the topic. New titles are always being released, and older titles have a way of being rediscovered. When you find a title that works for you, just add it to the list. This way you will have a relatively easy time when setting up the program and have easy access to the titles that work for you.

Adventure

Five Little Ducks, by Ian Beck
In the Tall, Tall Grass, by Denise Fleming
Little Elephant, by Miela Ford and Tana Hoban
Across the Stream, by Mirra Ginsburg
Whose Mouse Are You?, by Robert Kraus
Runaway Rabbit, by Ron Mans
Hello Toes! Hello Feet!, by Ann Whiteford Paul
The Chick and the Duckling, by V. Suteyev
Bug Hunt, by Neecy Twinem
I Went Walking, by Sue Williams

Animals

Animal Moves, by Dawn Apperley
Animal Noises, by Dawn Apperley
Come Out, Muskrats, by Jim Arnosky
Little Gorilla, by Ruth Bornstein
Good Night, Good Night, by Sandra Boynton
My Barn, by Craig Brown
The Golden Egg Book, by Margaret Brown
Blink Like an Owl, by Kate Burns
Waddle Like a Duck, by Kate Burns
Tail Toes Eyes Ears Nose, by Marilee Burton
From Head to Toe, by Eric Carle
One Red Rooster, by Kathleen Carroll
Says Who?, by David Carter
Peek a Moo!, by Marie Cimarusti
Old MacDonald Had a Farm, by Frances Cony
Ducks Fly, by Lydia Dabcovich
Honk!, by Chris Demarest
Are You My Daddy?, by Carla Dijs
Are You My Mommy?, by Carla Dijs
Is That an Elephant Over There?, by Rebecca Elgar
Ask Mr. Bear, by Marjorie Flack

Barnyard Banter, by Denise Fleming
In the Small, Small Pond, by Denise Fleming
In the Tall, Tall Grass, by Denise Fleming
The ABC Bunny, by Wanda Gag
And So Can I!, by Bill Gillham
Across the Stream, by Mirra Ginsburg
Asleep, Asleep, by Mirra Ginsburg
Oh, A-Hunting We Will Go, by John Langstaff
Over in the Meadow, by John Langstaff
Can You Hop?, by Lisa Lawston
The Owl and the Pussycat, by Edward Lear
Runaway Rabbit, by Ron Maris
Brown Bear, Brown Bear, by Bill Martin
I Love Animals, by Flora McDonnell
Toddlerobics Animal Fun, by Zita Newcome
As Quiet as a Mouse, by Hilda Offen
The Box with Red Wheels, by Maud and Miska Petersham
Little Bird, by Saviour Pirotta
Who Said Meow?, by Marie Polushkin
Sam Who Never Forgets, by Eve Rice
Hide and Seek, by Janet Morgan Stoeke
Rainy Day, by Janet Morgan Stoeke
The Chick and the Duckling, by V. Suteyev
This Is the Farmer, by Nancy Tafuri
Big Fat Worm, by Nancy Van Laan
Do Pigs Have Stripes?, by Melanie Walsh
I Went Walking, by Sue Williams
Let's Go Visiting, by Sue Williams
Dads Are Such Fun, by Jakki Wood

Animals—Farm

My Barn, by Craig Brown
One Red Rooster, by Kathleen Carroll
Peek a Moo!, by Marie Cimarusti
Old MacDonald Had a Farm, by Frances Cony
Honk!, by Chris Demarest
Barnyard Tracks, by Dee Dee Duffy
Barnyard Banter, by Denise Fleming
Good Morning, Chick, by Mirra Ginsburg
I Love Animals, by Flora McDonnell
The Box with Red Wheels, by Maud and Miska Petersham
Cock-a-Doodle-Doo!, by Venice Shone
Hide and Seek, by Janet Morgan Stoeke
Rainy Day, by Janet Morgan Stoeke
This Is the Farmer, by Nancy Tafuri

I Went Walking, by Sue Williams
Let's Go Visiting, by Sue Williams

Animals—Jungle

Little Gorilla, by Ruth Bornstein
Are You My Daddy?, by Carla Dijs
Is That an Elephant Over There?, by Rebecca Elgar
Little Elephant, by Miela Ford and Tana Hoban
Splash!, by Flora McDonnell
Dads Are Such Fun, by Jakki Wood

Babies

Baby in the Box, by Frank Asch
Mama Cat Has Three Kittens, by Denise Fleming
Pots and Pans, by Patricia Hubbel
I See, by Rachel Isadora
When You Were a Baby, by Ann Jonas
Whose Mouse Are You?, by Robert Kraus
Baby Loves, by Michael Lawrence
The Saucepan Game, by Jan Omerod
Clap Hands, by Helen Oxenbury
Tickle, Tickle, by Helen Oxenbury
The Box with Red Wheels, by Maud and Miska Petersham
On Mother's Lap, by Ann Scott
"More, More, More," Said the Baby, by Vera Williams

Bathtime

My Blue Boat, by Chris Demarest
I Love Boats, by Flora McDonnell
Tom and Pippo Go for a Walk, by Helen Oxenbury

Bears

Just Like Daddy, by Frank Asch
Panda Big and Panda Small, by Jane Cabrera
Sleepy Bear, by Lydia Dabcovich
Ask Mr. Bear, by Marjorie Flack
Bears, by Ruth Krauss
Where Is Alice's Bear?, by Fiona Pragoff
How Do I Put It On?, by Shigeo Wantanabe
The Little Mouse, the Red Ripe Strawberry and the Big Hungry Bear,
　by Don and Audrey Wood

Bedtime

Ten, Nine, Eight, by Molly Bang

Grandfather Twilight, by Barbara Berger
Busy Lizzie, by Holly Berry
Good Night, Good Night, by Sandra Boynton
Goodnight Moon, by Margaret Brown
Time for Bed, by Mem Fox
Asleep, Asleep, by Mirra Ginsburg
I Hear, by Rachel Isadora
Piggies, by Don and Audrey Wood

Birds

Little Robin Redbreast, by Shari Halpern
The Owl and the Pussycat, by Edward Lear
Little Bird, by Saviour Pirotta
Hide and Seek, by Janet Morgan Stoeke
Rainy Day, by Janet Morgan Stoeke
The Big Fat Worm, by Nancy Van Laan

Birthdays

Little Gorilla, by Ruth Bornstein
Ask Mr. Bear, by Marjorie Flack
Benny Bakes a Cake, by Eve Rice

Boats

My Blue Boat, by Chris Demarest
I Love Boats, by Flora McDonnell

Body Awareness

Busy Lizzie, by Holly Berry
Here Are My Hands, by Bill Martin
Toddlerobics, by Zita Newcome
Hello Toes! Hello Feet!, by Ann Whiteford Paul
Piggies, by Don and Audrey Wood

Bugs

In the Tall, Tall Grass, by Denise Fleming
Bug Hunt, by Neecy Twinem
The Big Fat Worm, by Nancy Van Laan

Cats

Along Came Toto, by Ann Axworthy
Just Like Jasper!, by Nick Butterworth
Mama Cat Has Three Kittens, by Denise Fleming
Little Robin Redbreast, by Shari Halpern
The Owl and the Pussycat, by Edward Lear

The Saucepan Game, by Jan Omerod
Who Said Meow?, by Marie Polushkin
The Big Fat Worm, by Nancy Van Laan

Chickens

Big Fat Hen, by Keith Baker
Across the Stream, by Mirra Ginsburg
Good Morning, Chick, by Mirra Ginsburg
Hide and Seek, by Janet Morgan Stoeke
Rainy Day, by Janet Morgan Stoeke
The Chick and the Duckling, by V. Suteyev

Clouds

The Little Cloud, by Eric Carle

Colors

Freight Train, by Donald Crews
Lunch, by Denise Fleming
Oh No, Anna!, by Vivian French and Alex Ayliffe
Rain, by Robert Kalan
Brown Bear, Brown Bear, by Bill Martin
My Many Colored Days, by Dr. Seuss

Concepts

I Like Books, by Anthony Browne
Panda Big and Panda Small, by Jane Cabrera
Bathwater's Hot, by Shirley Hughes
Blue Sea, by Robert Kalan,

Counting/Numbers

Big Fat Hen, by Keith Baker
Ten, Nine, Eight, by Molly Bang
Five Little Ducks, by Ian Beck
What's for Lunch?, by Eric Carle
One Red Rooster, by Kathleen Carroll
Over in the Meadow, by John Langstaff
Five Little Ducks, by Raffi
Let's Go Visiting, by Sue Williams

Daily Life

Baby Loves, by Michael Lawrence
Everything Has a Place, by Patricia Lillie

Dogs

Along Came Toto, by Ann Axworthy
Hunky Dory Ate It!, by Katie Evans
Hunky Dory Found It!, by Katie Evans
Where's Spot?, by Eric Hill
Who Said Meow?, by Marie Polushkin
Benny Bakes a Cake, by Eve Rice
The Big Fat Worm, by Nancy Van Laan

Ducks

Five Little Ducks, by Ian Beck
The Golden Egg Book, by Margaret Brown
Ducks Fly, by Lydia Dabcovich
Across the Stream, by Mirra Ginsburg
Five Little Ducks, by Raffi
Come Along Daisy!, by Jane Simmons
The Chick and the Duckling, by V. Suteyev
Have You Seen My Duckling?, by Nancy Tafuri

Elephants

Is That an Elephant Over There?, by Rebecca Elgar
Little Elephant, by Miela Ford and Tana Hoban
Splash!, by Flora McDonnell
Sam Who Never Forgets, by Eve Rice

Emotions

My Many Colored Days, by Dr.Seuss

Exercise

From Head to Toe, by Eric Carle
Toddlerobics, by Zita Newcome
Toddlerobics Animal Fun, by Zita Newcome

Exploring

Five Little Ducks, by Ian Beck
Oh No, Anna!, by Vivian French and Alex Ayliffe
Five Little Ducks, by Raffi
Come Along Daisy!, by Jane Simmons
Have You Seen My Duckling?, by Nancy Tafuri

Families

Just Like Daddy, by Frank Asch
Honk!, by Chris Demarest
Are You My Daddy?, by Carla Dijs

Are You My Mommy?, by Carla Dijs
Time for Bed, by Mem Fox
Titch, by Pat Hutchins
Whose Mouse Are You?, by Robert Kraus
Baby Loves, by Michael Lawrence
On Mother's Lap, by Ann Scott
Noisy Nora, by Rosemary Wells
"More, More, More," Said the Baby, by Vera Williams
Dads Are Such Fun, by Jakki Wood

Farms

My Barn, by Craig Brown
One Red Rooster, by Kathleen Carroll
Peek a Moo!, by Marie Cimarusti
Old MacDonald Had a Farm, by Frances Cony
Honk!, by Chris Demarest
Barnyard Tracks, by Dee Dee Duffy
Barnyard Banter, by Denise Fleming
Good Morning, Chick, by Mirra Ginsburg
I Love Animals, by Flora McDonnell
Cock-a-Doodle-Doo!, by Venice Shone
Hide and Seek, by Janet Morgan Stoeke
Rainy Day, by Janet Morgan Stoeke
This Is the Farmer, by Nancy Tafuri

Fathers

Just Like Daddy, by Frank Asch
Are You My Daddy?, by Carla Dijs
Dads Are Such Fun, by Jakki Wood

Fish

Blue Sea, by Robert Kalan

Food

What's for Lunch?, by Eric Carle
Hunky Dory Ate It!, by Katie Evans
Lunch, by Denise Fleming
Sam Who Never Forgets, by Eve Rice
The Little Mouse, the Red Ripe Strawberry and the Big Hungry Bear,
    by Don and Audrey Wood

Friends

Along Came Toto, by Ann Axworthy
I Like Me!, by Nancy Carlson

Games

Tail Toes Eyes Ears Nose, by Marilee Burton
Says Who?, by David Carter
Peek a Moo!, by Marie Cimarusti
Is That an Elephant Over There?, by Rebecca Elgar
Hunky Dory Found It!, by Katie Evans
Pots and Pans, by Patricia Hubbel
The Saucepan Game, by Jan Omerod
Tickle, Tickle, by Helen Oxenbury
Where Is Alice's Bear?, by Fiona Pragoff
Peek-a-Boo, by Matthew Price and Jean Claver
Hide and Seek, by Janet Morgan Stoeke
Rainy Day, by Janet Morgan Stoeke
Piggies, by Don and Audrey Wood

Gardens

Titch, by Pat Hutchins
The Carrot Seed, by Ruth Krauss
In My Garden, by Ron Maris

Getting Dressed

A Fox Got My Socks, by Hilda Offen
Look, There's My Hat!, by Maureen Roffey
How Do I Put It On?, by Shigeo Wantanabe

Growing Up

Little Gorilla, by Ruth Bornstein
When You Were a Baby, by Ann Jonas

Hats

Benny's Four Hats, by Ruth Jaynes
Whose Hat?, by Margaret Miller
Look, There's My Hat!, by Maureen Roffey

Holidays

The Five Little Pumpkins, by Iris Van Rynbach

Imagination

My Blue Boat, by Chris Demarest
The Saucepan Game, by Jan Omerod

Manners

Lunch, by Denise Fleming

Messes

Lunch, by Denise Fleming
Oh No, Anna!, by Vivian French and Alex Ayliffe
Pots and Pans, by Patricia Hubbel

Mice

Lunch, by Denise Fleming
Whose Mouse Are You?, by Robert Kraus
Gentle Rosie, by Mary Morgan
This Is the Farmer, by Nancy Tafuri
Noisy Nora, by Rosemary Wells
The Little Mouse, the Red Ripe Strawberry and the Big Hungry Bear,
    by Don and Audrey Wood

Monkeys

What's for Lunch?, by Eric Carle
Tom and Pippo Go for a Walk, by Helen Oxenbury
Tom and Pippo in the Snow, by Helen Oxenbury

Mothers

Honk!, by Chris Demarest
Are You My Mother?, by Carla Dijs
Ask Mr. Bear, by Marjorie Flack
Mama Cat Has Three Kittens, by Denise Fleming
On Mother's Lap, by Ann Scott
Come Along Daisy!, by Jane Simmons
Have You Seen My Duckling?, by Nancy Tafuri

Movable Books

(These have pop-up, pull-tab, flap, and other types of "active" pages)
Animal Moves, by Dawn Apperley
Animal Noises, by Dawn Apperley
Blink Like an Owl, by Kate Burns
Waddle Like a Duck, by Kate Burns
What's for Lunch?, by Eric Carle
Says Who?, by David Carter
Peek a Moo!, by Marie Cimarusti
Old MacDonald Had a Farm, by Frances Cony
What Can Rabbit See?, by Lucy Cousins
Honk!, by Chris Demarest
Are You My Daddy?, by Carla Dijs
Are You My Mommy?, by Carla Dijs
Is That an Elephant Over There?, by Rebecca Elgar
Where's Spot?, by Eric Hill

Trucks and Other Working Wheels, by Jan Pienkowski
Where Is Alice's Bear?, by Fiona Pragoff
Peek-a-Boo, by Matthew Price and Jean Claver
Bug Hunt, by Neecy Twinem

Movement

Animal Moves, by Dawn Apperley
Animal Noises, by Dawn Apperley
Busy Lizzie, by Holly Berry
Blink Like an Owl, by Kate Burns
Waddle Like a Duck, by Kate Burns
From Head to Toe, by Eric Carle
Clap Your Hands, by Lorinda Cauley
And So Can I!, by Bill Gillham
Bouncing, by Shirley Hughes
Toddlerobics, by Zita Newcome
Toddlerobics Animal Fun, by Zita Newcome
As Quiet as a Mouse, by Hilda Offen
Little Bird, by Saviour Pirotta
The Ball Bounced, by Nancy Tafuri

Occupations

Whose Hat?, by Margaret Miller
Sam Who Never Forgets, by Eve Rice

Outside

In the Small, Small Pond, by Denise Fleming
In the Tall, Tall Grass, by Denise Fleming
Tom and Pippo Go for a Walk, by Helen Oxenbury
Tom and Pippo in the Snow, by Helen Oxenbury
Bug Hunt, by Neecy Twinem
I Went Walking, by Sue Williams

Participation

(These encourage group to join in with actions and/or with the text)
Animal Moves, by Dawn Apperley
Animal Noises, by Dawn Apperley
Busy Lizzie, by Holly Berry
Marc Brown's Favorite Hand Rhymes, by Marc Brown
Blink Like an Owl, by Kate Burns
Waddle Like a Duck, by Kate Burns
From Head to Toe, by Eric Carle
Clap Your Hands, by Lorinda Cauley
Knock at the Door and Other Baby Action Rhymes, by Kay Chorao

Oh No, Anna!, by Vivian French and Alex Ayliffe
And So Can I!, by Bill Gillham
Can You Hop?, by Lisa Lawston
Brown Bear, Brown Bear, by Bill Martin
Toddlerobics, by Zita Newcome
Toddlerobics Animal Fun, by Zita Newcome
A Fox Got My Socks, by Hilda Offen
As Quiet as a Mouse, by Hilda Offen
Little Bird, by Saviour Pirotta
Piggies, by Don and Audrey Wood

Pigs

I Like Me!, by Nancy Carlson
Do Pigs Have Stripes?, by Melanie Walsh
Piggies, by Don and Audrey Wood

Play

Baby in the Box, by Frank Asch
Busy Lizzie, by Holly Berry
Clap Your Hands, by Lorinda Cauley
Bounce, Bounce, Bounce, by Kathy Henderson
Pots and Pans, by Patricia Hubbel
Bouncing, by Shirley Hughes
The Saucepan Game, by Jan Omerod
Hide and Seek, by Janet Morgan Stoeke
Rainy Day, by Janet Morgan Stoeke

Poetry

Marc Brown's Favorite Hand Rhymes, by Marc Brown
Knock at the Door and Other Baby Action Rhymes, by Kay Chorao
Mary Had a Little Lamb, by Sarah Hale
Little Robin Redbreast, by Shari Halpern
The Owl and the Pussycat, by Edward Lear
Catch Me and Kiss Me and Say It Again, by Clyde Watson

Rabbits

The Golden Egg Book, by Margaret Brown
Goodnight Moon, by Margaret Brown
Home for a Bunny, by Margaret Brown
What Can Rabbit See?, by Lucy Cousins
The ABC Bunny, by Wanda Gag
Runaway Rabbit, by Ron Maris

Rain

The Little Cloud, by Eric Carle
Who Is Tapping at My Window?, by A. G. Deming
Rain, by Robert Kalan

Response Books

(These titles encourage the listeners to respond verbally to the text)
Tail Toes Eyes Ears Nose, by Marilee Burton
If You're Happy and You Know It, Clap Your Hands, by David Carter
Says Who?, by David Carter
Are You My Daddy?, by Carla Dijs
Are You My Mommy?, by Carla Dijs
Barnyard Tracks, by Dee Dee Duffy
Is That an Elephant Over There?, by Rebecca Elgar
Barnyard Banter, by Denise Fleming
Where's Spot?, by Eric Hill
Benny's Four Hats, by Ruth Jaynes,
Brown Bear, Brown Bear, by Bill Martin
Peek-a-Boo, by Matthew Price and Jean Claver
Bug Hunt, by Neecy Twinem
Do Pigs Have Stripes?, by Melanie Walsh
I Went Walking, by Sue Williams
Let's Go Visiting, Sue Williams

Rhyming Story

Baby in the Box, by Frank Asch
Big Fat Hen, by Keith Baker
Ten, Nine, Eight, by Molly Bang
Five Little Ducks, by Ian Beck
Good Night, Good Night, by Sandra Boynton
Goodnight Moon, by Margaret Brown
I Like Books, by Anthony Browne
Panda Big and Panda Small, by Jane Cabrera
One Red Rooster, by Kathleen Carroll
If You're Happy and You Know It, Clap Your Hands, by David Carter
Clap Your Hands, by Lorinda Cauley
Who Is Tapping at My Window?, by A. G. Deming
Hunky Dory Ate It!, by Katie Evans
Hunky Dory Found It!, by Katie Evans
Barnyard Banter, by Denise Fleming
In the Small, Small Pond, by Denise Fleming
In the Tall, Tall Grass, by Denise Fleming
Time for Bed, by Mem Fox
The ABC Bunny, by Wanda Gag

Mary Had a Little Lamb, by Sarah Hale
Little Robin Redbreast, by Shari Halpern
Bounce, Bounce, Bounce, by Kathy Henderson
Bathwater's Hot, by Shirley Hughes
Bears, by Ruth Krauss
Oh, A-Hunting We Will Go, by John Langstaff
Over in the Meadow, by John Langstaff
The Owl and the Pussycat, by Edward Lear
Chugga-Chugga Choo-Choo, by Kevin Lewis
Brown Bear, Brown Bear, by Bill Martin
Here Are My Hands, by Bill Martin
Toddlerobics, by Zita Newcome
Toddlerobics Animal Fun, by Zita Newcome
A Fox Got My Socks, by Hilda Offen
As Quiet as a Mouse, by Hilda Offen
Hello Toes! Hello Feet!, by Ann Whiteford Paul
My Many Colored Days, by Dr. Seuss
Sheep in a Jeep, by Nancy Shaw
The Five Little Pumpkins, by Iris Van Rynbach
Noisy Nora, by Rosemary Wells
I Went Walking, by Sue Williams
Let's Go Visiting, by Sue Williams

Seasons

Sleepy Bear, by Lydia Dabcovich
In the Small, Small Pond, by Denise Fleming
Tom and Pippo in the Snow, by Helen Oxenbury
The Five Little Pumpkins, by Iris Van Rynbach

Senses

What Can Rabbit See?, by Lucy Cousins
I Hear, by Rachel Isadora
I See, by Rachel Isadora

Shapes

The Little Cloud, by Eric Carle

Sheep

Mary Had a Little Lamb, by Sarah Hale
Sheep in a Jeep, by Nancy Shaw

Size

Little Gorilla, by Ruth Bornstein
Panda Big and Panda Small, by Jane Cabrera

Blue Sea, by Robert Kalan
Look, There's My Hat!, by Maureen Roffey

Songs

The Five Little Ducks, by Ian Beck
If You're Happy and You Know It, Clap Your Hands, by David Carter
Old MacDonald Had a Farm, by Frances Cony
Mary Had a Little Lamb, by Sarah Hale
Oh, A-Hunting We Will Go, by John Langstaff
Over in the Meadow, by John Langstaff
Five Little Ducks, by Raffi

Sounds

Animal Noises, by Dawn Apperley
My Barn, by Craig Brown
Says Who?, by David Carter
Peek a Moo!, by Marie Cimarusti
Honk!, by Chris Demarest
Barnyard Banter, by Denise Fleming
Pots and Pans, by Patricia Hubbel
I Hear, by Rachel Isadora
Clap Hands, by Helen Oxenbury
Tickle, Tickle, by Helen Oxenbury
Who Said Meow?, by Marie Polushkin
Noisy Nora, by Rosemary Wells

Things That Go

Freight Train, by Donald Crews
My Blue Boat, by Chris Demarest
Chugga-Chugga Choo-Choo, by Kevin Lewis
I Love Boats, by Flora McDonnell
Trucks and Other Working Wheels, by Jan Pienkowski
Sheep in a Jeep, by Nancy Shaw

Toys

Just Like Jasper!, by Nick Butterworth
Titch, by Pat Hutchins
Now We Can Go, by Ann Jonas
Chugga-Chugga Choo-Choo, by Kevin Lewis
Tom and Pippo Go for a Walk, by Helen Oxenbury
Tom and Pippo in the Snow, by Helen Oxenbury
The Ball Bounced, by Nancy Tafuri

Trains

Freight Train, by Donald Crews
Chugga-Chugga Choo-Choo, by Kevin Lewis

Water

Come Out, Muskrats, by Jim Arnosky
My Blue Boat, by Chris Demarest
In the Small, Small Pond, by Denise Fleming
Little Elephant, by Miela Ford and Tana Hoban
Across the Stream, by Mirra Ginsburg
Blue Sea, by Robert Kalan
I Love Boats, by Flora McDonnell
Splash!, by Flora McDonnell
Have You Seen My Duckling?, by Nancy Tafuri

Weather

The Little Cloud, by Eric Carle
Who Is Tapping at My Window?, by A. G. Deming
Benny's Four Hats, by Ruth Jaynes
Rain, by Robert Kalan

NURSERY RHYMES AND FINGERPLAYS

Nursery rhymes and fingerplays should be an intrinsic part of child-hood and are one of the first language-building experiences for most children. Adults who did not have exposure to them as children may find them silly and are sometimes embarrassed when doing them. Rhymes, however, are an important part of language development and of the child's background knowledge. The child will meet allusions to these rhymes throughout adult life. Children learn by listening and doing. By actively engaging the child, the adult not only helps the child learn about language but also shares in the experience.

Rhymes also help the child develop the skills of listening, compre-hending directions, and acting on them. Children need to develop lis-tening skills before they have comprehension and reading skills. Since repetition of rhymes usually takes place, the participants become fa-miliar with them and thus gain confidence in their own ability to speak and act out the rhyme for themselves.

When using rhymes in this program, use a core collection of famil-iar rhymes at each program that can be put on a handout to go home with the participants. This way they can learn them and/or repeat them on their own. It will lessen the pressure to remember everything that takes place during the program and encourage them to continue the language experience at home. Children and adults will recognize familiar rhymes and be less hesitant to try unfamiliar rhymes if only a few new ones are introduced at a time.

How does one teach a rhyme or fingerplay? I suggest that you treat it as being new to the entire group, especially at programs where there are different cultures and languages present. Speak clearly, and use simple terms as you demonstrate the actions. The three methods I have found to work well are:

1. The presenter says the desired rhyme/fingerplay in its entirety, demonstrating the actions that go with it at the same time. It is then repeated with the whole group.
2. The presenter says a line and demonstrates the action. The entire group repeats the line and the action required. After the whole rhyme is presented this way the entire group does the whole rhyme/fingerplay straight through.
3. Use an audiotape or CD to support the presenter. This way the presenter can act along with the group to learn the rhyme. *The Baby Record* by Bob McGrath and Katherine Smithrim is one example of a good one.

Learning the words to rhymes and fingerplays can be done in various ways. In addition to a handout, you can display a poster with the words clearly written in large letters in the front of the room. Do not rely on these printed posters and sheets any longer than necessary, however, since the adults will often focus attention on reading the words instead of on the child. Large paper pads can hold numerous rhymes printed out large enough for a group. Be sure to mark the ones you plan to use ahead of time—perhaps by tacking a sticky note on it or using a paper clip. This way you will not have to search through pages to find the rhyme you want. Make sure that the pad can be displayed without problems on an easel or table.

There are various ways to say and act out rhymes. Rhymes and fingerplays are often adapted to the speed or verbal skill of the person doing them. The adults can share their versions, with the presenter encouraging their own creativity in using body language. Even familiar rhymes can be presented in a new light when the whole body is used instead of just fingers or toes for "This Little Piggy."

Quiet often there is an age span for children in this program, which results in the presence of different developmental levels. Some children may be precrawlers, others nonstop movers. Many adults may feel their child is not actively participating or paying strict attention.

It is best to remember to reassure the adults that the children are receiving or being made aware of words, rhythm, and rhyme by just being there. Introducing the world of language and literature to children at an early age gives them a greater chance to develop their skills of listening and comprehension. Children must first be exposed to the world of language in order to learn about it. They learn by observing and absorbing the experiences around them. Slowly, they will begin to participate at their own pace and when they are ready. (Ernst, 1995: p. 48)

Rhymes are often put to tunes and therefore may be defined also as songs or chants. The following list of rhymes, fingerplays, and songs is in no way complete but contains a sampling of familiar and traditional rhymes, fingerplays, and songs available. In the section following the list are theme programs. These combine the books, rhymes, fingerplays, and songs for each theme listed. The rhymes in that section that are not included in the written out list are given sources to facilitate looking them up. These additional resources can be found at the end of chapter 4 and in the resource list for music in chapter 5.

Nursery Rhymes, Fingerplays, and Songs

Abranlas, Cierrenlas (Open, Shut Them)

Abranlas, cierrenlas		Open, shut them.
	(open, close hands)	
Abranlas, cierrenlas,		Open, shut them.
	(open, close hands)	
Pla, pla, pla, pla, pla.		Give a little clap,
	(clap hands)	
Abranlas, cierrenlas,		Open, shut them.
	(open, close hands)	
Abranlas, cierrenlas,		Open, shut them.
	(open, close hands)	
Pongalas aca.		Put them in your lap.
	(fold hands in lap)	

Acka Backa

Acka backa soda cracker,
Acka backa boo.
 (rock, swing, or bounce child)
Acka backa soda cracker,
I love you.

(pick up and give child a hug)
Acka backa soda cracker,
Acka backa boo.
    (rock, swing, or bounce child)
Acka backa soda cracker,
Up goes you!
    (lift child up into the air)

All Around the Mulberry Bush

    ("mulberry bush" can be changed to "cobbler's bench")
All around the mulberry bush,
the monkey chased the weasel.
The monkey thought 'twas all in fun—
POP! Goes the weasel.

All for Baby

Here's a ball for baby,
    (touch fingertips, forming ball)
Big and soft and round.
Here is baby's hammer,
    (pound one fist on other)
Oh, how he can pound.
Here is baby's music
    (clap hands)
Clapping, clapping so.
Here are baby's soldiers
    (hold ten fingers erect)
Standing in a row.
Here is baby's trumpet
    (one fist in front of the other at mouth)
Toot, too, too, too, too.
Here's the way that baby
Plays at peek-a-boo.
    (spread fingers in front of eyes)
Here's a big umbrella
    *(hold index finger of right hand erect, place palm of left hand
      on top of finger; youngest can put hands over head)*
To keep the baby dry.
Here is baby's cradle,
    (cross arms)
Rock-a-baby bye.
    (rock back and forth)

Apple Tree

Way up high in an apple tree,
(*hold arms above head, fingers spread*)
Two little apples did I see.
(*make fists*)
So I shook that tree as hard as I could,
(*wiggle entire body*)
Down, came the apples.
(*lower arms*)
Mmmmm, they were good!
(*rub tummy*)

Baa, Baa, Black Sheep

(*works as a flannel-board presentation; if sung, repeat first two
lines at end*)
Baa, baa, black sheep, have you any wool?
Yes, sir, yes sir, three bags full.
One for my master and one for my dame,
and one for the little boy who lives down the lane.

Baby's Nap

This is a baby ready for a nap.
(*hold up finger*)
Lay him down in his mother's lap.
(*place in palm of hand*)
Cover him up so he won't peep.
(*wrap other fingers to cover him*)
Rock him 'til he's fast asleep.
(*rock hands to and fro*)

Beehive

Here is the little beehive.
(*hold up fist*)
Where are the bees?
Hidden away where nobody sees.
Soon they come creeping out of the hive.
One, two, three, four, five.
(*open fist slowly then tickle child on five*)

Bend and Stretch

(*suit actions to words*)
Bend and stretch, reach for the stars.
There goes Jupiter, here comes Mars.
Bend and stretch, reach for the sky.
Stand on tip-e-toe, oh! So high!

Bingo

(*clapping song, walk in circle holding child and move toward center one step with each letter; can also do this in front of a mirror.*)
There was a farmer had a dog and Bingo was his name-o.
B-I-N-G-O,
B-I-N-G-O,
B-I-N-G-O,
and Bingo was his name-o.

Choo-Choo Train

This is a choo-choo train
(*bend arms at elbows*)
Puffing down the track.
(*rotate arms in rhythm*)
Now it's going forward,
(*step forward*)
Now it's going back.
(*step back*)
Now the bell is ringing,
(*pull bell cord with closed fist or tap child's nose gently*)
Now the whistle blows.
(*hold fist near mouth and nose or blow on child's head*)
What a lot of noise it makes
(*cover ears*)
Everywhere it goes.
(*stretch out arms*)

Cinco Calabacitas (Five Little Pumpkins)
(Note: Since children have difficulty holding up fingers, this works as a flannel-board story also.)

Cinco calabacitas sentadas en un porton.　　　Five little pumpkins sitting on a gate;
(*cross hands and use one hand, five fingers for five pumpkins*)

La primera dijo:	The first one said,
(hold up finger)	
"Se esta haciendo tarde."	"My, it's getting late."
La segunda dijo:	The second one said,
(hold up second finger)	
"Hay brujas en el aire."	"There are witches in the air."
La tercera dijo:	The third one said,
(hold up third finger	
"No le hace."	"But we don't care."
La cuarta dijo:	The fourth one said,
(hold up fourth finger)	
"Corramos, corramos!"	"Let's run, let's run!"
La quinta dijo:	The fifth one said,
(hold up thumb)	
"Es una noche de espanto."	"It's Halloween fun."
Uuuu hizo el veinto	"WOOOOOOOOO," went the wind,
(wave arms)	
Y se apagaron las luces.	And out went the lights.
(clap)	
Las cinco calabacitas	These five little pumpkins
Corrieron a esconderse!	Ran fast out of sight!
(run fingers behind back)	

Clap Your Hands

Clap your hands, one, two, three
  (clap hands on one, two, three)
Clap your hands, just like me!
  (clap on last three words)

Other verse variations include: roll your hands, wave your hands, nod your head, and other body motions.

Cobbler, Cobbler

Cobbler, cobbler, mend my shoe.
Give it one stitch, give it two,
Give it three, give it four,
And if it needs it, give it more.
  (pat shoe or foot, have child pat adult's)

Criss, Cross, Applesauce

Criss, cross, applesauce
  (draw an X on child's back with finger)

Spiders running up your back
     (*walk fingers up child's back*)
Cool breeze
     (*blow gently on child's neck and back of head*)
Tight squeeze
     (*give child a big hug*)
Now you've got the shivers!
     (*tickle child gently all over*)

Dance to Your Daddy

Dance to your daddy, my little laddy,
Dance to your daddy, my little lamb.
You shall have a fishy in a little dishy,
You shall have a fishy when the boat comes in.

Dos Pajaritos (Two Little Birds)
(see also *Two Little Black Birds*)

Dos pajaritos muy sentados
     (*extend two index fingers*)
Enuna cerca muy alta:
Vuela Panchito, vuela Pedrito.
 	
     (*fly hands behind back*)
Vuelve Panchito, vuelve Pedrito.
	Two little birds
	
	Sitting on a fence;
	Panchito flys away,
	Pedrito flys away.
	
	Panchito returns,
	Pedrito returns.

     (*return hands to front with index finger still extended*)

Down by the Station

Down by the station, early in the morning,
See the little puffer-bellies all in a row;
See the station master pull the little handle—
Chugg, chugg, toot, toot, off we go!

Drums

Boom! Boom! Boom!
Goes the big brass drum.
Tat-a-tat-tat goes the little one.
And down the street in line we come
To the boom, boom, boom
Of the big brass drum,
And the rat-a-tat-tat of the little one.
     (*pound one fist on the palm of the other hand throughout*)

The Eentsy, Weentsy Spider: see *The Great Big Spider*

The Engine

Here is an engine
That runs on this track.
>   *(use left arm for track and right hand for engine that runs up
>   arm)*
It whistles—"Toot Toot"
And then it runs back.
>   *(run fingers back down)*

Father and Mother and Uncle John: see *Mother and Father and Uncle
John*

Fee Fi Fo Fum

Fee, fie, fo fum
>   *(point to fingers, one by one)*
see my fingers,
>   *(wiggle fingers)*
see my thumbs.
>   *(wiggle thumbs)*
Fee, fie, fo, fum
fingers gone—
now the thumbs.
>   *(wiggle fingers and thumbs then hide behind back)*

Fishies
(Reprinted with permission. *Plant A Little Seed, Songs for Growing
Children*, Nancy Stewart).

There are so many fishies in the deep blue sea. What color fishy do
>   you see?
Red, red, this one's red. This little fishy is red.
>   *(cut out five fish shapes in different-colored felt, change color
>   to match song)*
There are so many fishies in the deep blue sea.
Can you count the fishies with me . . . 1,2,3,4,5.

Five Little Pumpkins
(see also *Cinco Calabacitas*)

Five little pumpkins sitting on a gate.

     (*hold up five fingers*)
The first one said, "My, it's getting late."
     (*hold up one finger then point to wrist*)
The second one said, "There are witches in the air."
     (*hold up two fingers, wave hand in air*)
The third one said, "I don't care!"
     (*hold up three fingers and shake head "no"*)
The fourth one said, "Let's run and run and run."
     (*hold up four fingers and pump arms as if running*)
The fifth one said, "I'm ready for some fun."
     (*hold five fingers up, then point to self*)
Ooooooh went the wind,
Out went the light.
     (*clap hands*)
And the five little pumpkins rolled out of sight.
     (*roll hands*)

Five Plump Peas

Five plump peas in a pea pod pressed.
     (*hold one fist up*)
One grew, two grew, and so did all the rest.
     (*open fist one finger at a time*)
They grew and they grew and they never stopped.
     (*putting both hands together move them apart on each "grew"*
They grew so big that the pea pod popped!
     (*clap hands on "popped"*)

From Wibbleton to Wobbleton
(fun to clap to or use as a bouncing rhyme)

From Wibbleton to Wobbleton is fifteen miles,
From Wobbleton to Wibbleton is fifteen miles,
From Wibbleton to Wobbleton, from Wobbleton to Wibbleton,
From Wibbleton to Wobbleton is fifteen miles.

Gack-Goon

"Gack-goon," went the little green frog one day.
     (*clap or open hands on each "Gack-goon"*)
"Gack-goon," went the little green frog.
"Gack-goon," went the little green frog one day.
And his eyes went "Gack-gack-goon."

The Grand Old Duke of York
(great marching rhyme)

The grand old Duke of York,
He had ten thousand men.
He marched them up to the top of the hill,
And he marched them down again.
And when they were up, they were up,
And when they were down, they were down,
And when they were only halfway up,
They were neither up nor down.
> (*hop up on last line*)

Grandma's Spectacles

These are Grandma's spectacles,
> (*bring index finger and thumb together and place against face*)

This is Grandma's hat.
> (*bring fingers together in a peak over head*)

This is the way she folds her hands,
> (*clasp hands together*)

And lays them in her lap.
> (*put hands in lap*)

Gray Squirrel

Gray Squirrel, gray squirrel,
Swish your bushy tail.
> (*child on adult's lap, swing knees side to side*)

Gray squirrel, gray squirrel,
Swish your bushy tail.
Wrinkle up your little nose,
> (*tap child's nose*)

Hold a nut between your toes.
> (*tickle child's toes*)

Gray squirrel, gray squirrel,
Swish your bushy tail.
> (*swing knees side to side*)

The Great Big Spider

The great big spider went up the water spout.
> (*standing, move arms and legs in a climbing motion*)

Down came the rain and washed the spider out.
> (*drop arms down and swing back and forth*)

Out came the sun and dried up all the rain,
(raise arms in circle over head)
And the great big spider went up the spout again.
(standing move arms and legs in a climbing motion)

Head and Shoulders, Knees and Toes

Head and shoulders, knees and toes,
(throughout, touch appropriate part of own body or child's body)
Knees and toes, knees and toes.
Head and shoulders, knees, and toes.
Eyes, ears, mouth, and nose.

Here Comes a Mouse

Here comes a mouse, mousie, mousie, mouse.
(wiggle fingers by child)
On tiny light feet and a soft pink nose,
tickle, tickle, wherever he goes.
(tickle child)
He'll run up your arm and under your chin,
(run fingers up child's arm to chin)
Don't open your mouth or the mouse will run in!
Mousie, mousie, mouse.
(child will almost always open mouth; tap chin, nose, or lips on last three words)

Here Is a Beehive

Here is a beehive,
(hold up a fist)
Where are the bees?
(shrug shoulders)
Hidden inside where nobody sees.
(point to fist)
Soon they'll come out, out of the hive,
One-two-three-four-five.
(slowly unfold fingers and on five give tickle)

Here Is a Bunny

Here is a bunny with ears so funny,
(one-hand fist with two fingers straight up)
And here's his hole in the ground.

(*put hand on waist, bent elbow*)
When a noise he hears,
(*cup hand to ear*)
He picks up his ears,
And jumps in his hole in the ground.
(*jump up in air or hop rabbit into hole*)

Here Is a Choo Choo Train
(Reprinted with permission, *Little Songs for Little Me,* Stewart)

Here is a choo choo train chugging down the tracks
(*bend arms at elbows and rotate arms*)
Now it's going faster, now the bell is ringing,
(*pretend to ring bell*)
Now the whistle blows
(*pretend to blow whistle*)
What a lot of noise it makes, everywhere it goes!
(*cover ears and shake head*)

Here Is the Engine

(*can hold up fingers in order, starting with thumb, or make
into a flannel-board story*)
Here is the engine on the track.
Here is the coal car, just in back.
Here is the boxcar to carry freight,
Here is the mail car. Don't be late!
Way back here at the end of the train
Rides the caboose through the sun and rain.

Here's a Ball

Here's a ball,
(*form circle with two hands*)
And here's a ball.
(*move hands apart*)
And a great big ball I see.
(*form large circle with arms*)
Shall we count them?
Are you ready?
One, two three!
(*repeat shapes*)

Here's a Cup

Here's a cup and here's a cup.
 (*make cup shape with hands or just hold up fists*)
And here's a pot of tea.
 (*cup hands together or pop up one thumb*)
Pour a cup and pour a cup,
 (*make pouring motion*)
and have a cup with me.
 (*drinking motion*)

Here We Go 'Round the Mulberry Bush:
see *All Around the Mulberry Bush*

Here We Go Up—Up—Up

Here we go up—up—up.
 (*move child by lifting and lowering, or have adult cross legs
  and sit child on foot*)
And here we go down—down—down.
And here we go back—and—forth and back—and—forth.
And here we go around and around and around.

Hey Diddle, Diddle

Hey diddle, diddle, the cat and the fiddle,
The cow jumped over the moon.
The little dog laughed to see such fun,
And the dish ran away with the spoon.

Hickety, Pickety My Black Hen

Hickety, pickety my black hen,
She lays eggs for gentlemen.
Gentlemen come every day
To see what my black hen doth lay.

Hickory, Dickory Dock

Hickory, dickory, dock,
 (*clasp hands together and swing gently back and forth*)
The mouse ran up the clock.
 (*run fingers up so hands end up above head*)
The clock struck one,
 (*clap hands once*)

The mouse ran down,
> (*bring arms back down in front*)
Hickory, dickory dock.
> (*clasp hands and swing gently back and forth*)
> (*can also run fingers up child's arm and touch nose on "one"*)

How Much Is That Doggie in the Window?
(this is fun to use with rhythm instruments such as shakers, or as a clapping song)

How much is that doggie in the window?
The one with the waggily tail.
How much is that doggie in the window?
I do hope that doggie's for sale!
Woof! Woof!

Humpty Dumpty

Humpty Dumpty sat on a wall.
> (*bounce child gently on lap or sit on floor with child on raised knees*)
Humpty Dumpty had a great fall.
All the king's horses and all the king's men,
Couldn't put Humpty together again.
> (*part legs, or straighten them to slide child down when Humpty falls*)

If You're Happy and You Know It

If you're happy and you know it clap your hands.
If you're happy and you know it clap your hands.
If you're happy and you know it then your face will surely show it.
> (*frame face with hands*)
If you're happy and you know it clap your hands.
> (*clap hands, tickle belly, pat head, and the like*)
If You're Wearing [color] Today
If you're wearing red today,
Red today, red today.
If you're wearing red today,
Please stand up!
> (*clap hands and have child stand alone or supported when asked; colors may vary*)

I Hear Thunder
(sung to *Frere Jacques*)

I hear thunder,
I hear thunder.
    (*pound hands gently on floor or lap*)
Hark, don't you?
    (*cup one hand by ear to listen*)
Hark, don't you?
    (*cup other hand by ear to listen*)
Pitter, patter raindrops,
Pitter, patter raindrops,
    (*wiggle fingers in falling motion in front of face*)
I'm wet through,
    (*shake body*)
So are you!
    (*point to child or give child a little tickle*)

I'll Drive a Dump Truck
(Reprinted with permission, *Little Songs for Little Me*, Stewart)
(Note: hold up pictures of what you're singing about, such as truck or car)

I'll drive a dump truck, dump truck, dump truck.
    (*hold hands as if on a steering wheel, or slap thighs in rhythm*)
I'll drive a dump truck all day long.
    (*repeat with school bus, airplane, fire truck, choo choo train, tugboat, and so on*)

I'm a Little Teapot

I'm a little teapot short and stout.
Here is my handle,
    (*put one hand on hip*)
Here is my spout.
    (*put other hand up in the air*)
When I get all steamed up,
Hear me shout.
Tip me over and pour me out.
    (*bend over at waist to the side then stand upright again*)
I'm a special teapot, it is true.
Here, let me show you what I can do.
I can change my handle and my spout,
    (*switch positions of arms*)
Tip me over and pour me out.
    (*bend to other side at waistline*)

It's Raining, It's Pouring

It's raining, it's pouring,
The old man is snoring.
Bumped his head,
And he went to bed,
And he didn't get up 'til the morning.

Jack and Jill

Jack and Jill went up the hill
To fetch a pail of water,
Jack fell down and broke his crown,
And Jill came tumbling after.

Jack Be Nimble

Jack be nimble,
　　　(*bounce child on lap*)
Jack be quick.
Jack jump over the candlestick.
　　　(*lift child up*)

Jack in the Box

Jack in the box, you sit so still
　　　(*kneel on floor with head covered by arms or hands*)
Won't you come out? Yes, I will!
　　　(*pop up on last phrase*)

Johnny Hammers One Hammer

Johnny hammers one hammer, one hammer, one hammer.
　　　(*pat one hand on leg to beat*)
Johnny hammers with one hammer all day long.
Johnny hammers with two hammers, two hammers, two hammers.
　　　(*pump both hands up and down*)
Johnny hammers with two hammers all day long.
　　　(*add feet for three and four hammers*)

Leg over Leg

Leg over leg
　　　(*child on lap, bounce or move legs back and forth*)
The dog went to Dover

When he came to a stile . . . .
Jump! He went over.
    (*dramatic pause before jump and lift child up*)

Little Boy Blue, Come Blow Your Horn
(see Sierra, 1997, for great ideas)

Little boy blue, come blow your horn.
The sheep's in the meadow, the cow's in the corn.
Where is the boy who looks after the sheep?
He's under the haystack fast asleep.
Will you wake him?
No, not I, for if I do he's sure to cry.

Little Miss Muffet

Little Miss Muffet sat on a tuffet,
Eating her curds and whey.
Along came a spider and sat down beside her
And frightened Miss Muffet away.

Little Turtle
(by Vachel Lindsay)

There was a little turtle,
    (*make a fist*)
He lived in a box.
    (*put one fist in cupped opposite hand*)
He swam in a puddle,
    (*make paddling motion with hands*)
He climbed on the rock.
    (*climb hands upwards in front of body*)
He snapped at a mosquito,
    (*make "snap" motion—touch fingers to thumb—on last word*)
He snapped at a flea,
    (*"snap" on last word*)
He snapped at a minnow.
    (*"snap" on last word*)
He snapped at me.
    (*"snap" on last word by your nose*)
He caught the mosquito,
    (*clap on last word*)
He caught the flea.
    (*clap on last word*)
He caught the minnow.
    (*clap on last word*)

But he didn't catch me!
        (*point to self and shake head, "no!"*)

Note: the youngest children may simply open and close hand for "snap" motion.

Lots of Cars
(Reprinted with permission, *Plant a Little Seed*, by Stewart)

There are lots of cars driving down the street
        (*hands as if on steering wheel, turning back and forth*)
Tell me what color do you see.
        (*on flannel board, place car shape in felt or use a picture*)
Big cars,
        (*spread arms wide apart*)
Little cars,
        (*bring hands close together*)
Beep, beep, beep.
        (*hand taps nose three times*)
        (*repeat using different-colored cars*)

Mary Had a Little Lamb

Mary had a little lamb,
Little lamb, little lamb.
Mary had a little lamb,
Its fleece was white as snow.
He followed her to school one day,
School one day, school one day.
He followed her to school one day,
Which was against the rule.
It made the children laugh and play,
Laugh and play, laugh and play.
It make the children laugh and play,
To see a lamb at school.

Mary, Mary Quite Contrary
(present as flannel-board story)

Mary, Mary quite contrary,
How does your garden grow?
With silver bells and cockle shells,
And pretty maids all in a row.

Mr. Turkey and Mr. Duck
(Reprinted with permission, *Little Songs for Little Me*, Stewart)

   (*start with hands behind back*)
Mr. Turkey went out one day in bright sunshiny weather.
   (*move one hand to front*)
He met Mr. Duck along the way.
   (*other hand comes out*)
They stopped to talk together.
   (*hands move up and down*)
Gobble, gobble, gobble, quack, quack, quack.
Gobble, gobble, gobble, quack, quack, quack.
   (*hands alternate moving during sounds, one turkey, other duck*)
And then they both went back, QUACK!
   (*hands go behind back, "duck" one sneaks out for last quack*)

Mother and Father and Uncle John

Mother and Father and Uncle John went to town one by one.
   (*bounce child in lap*)
Mother fell off.
   (*tip child to side on "off"*)
And Father fell off.
   (*tip child to other side on "off"*)
But Uncle John went on and on and on and on and on!
   (*lots of bounces on last line*)

My Pony Macaroni

I have a little pony,
   (*bounce child on knees throughout*)
His name is Macaroni.
He trots and trots and then he STOPS.
   (*pause*)
My funny little pony,
Mac-a-ro-ni!
   (*give child a jiggle on "ro," resume bounce*)

My Wiggles

   (*suit actions to words, adult can do to child*)
I wiggle my fingers.
I wiggle my toes.
I wiggle my shoulders.
I wiggle my nose.

Now the wiggles are out of me,
And I'm just as still as I can be.

Old MacDonald Had a Farm

Old MacDonald had a farm, e-i-e-i-o.
And on his farm he had a duck, e-i-e-i-o.
With a quack, quack here and a quack, quack there.
Here a quack, there a quack, everywhere a quack, quack.
Old MacDonald had a farm, e-i-e-i-o.
    (use other animals and sounds)

(Ideas: use stuffed toy animals and pull out of a bag or stick animal
puppets)

One, Two, Buckle My Shoe
(bouncing rhyme)

One, two, buckle my shoe,
Three, four, shut the door,
Five, six, pick up sticks,
Seven, eight, lay them straight,
Nine, ten, a big, fat hen.

Open, Shut Them

Open, shut them. Open, shut them.
    (open and close fist)
Give a little clap.
    (clap)
Open, shut them. Open shut them.
    (open and close fist)
Lay them in your lap.
    (put in lap)
Creep them, creep them,
creep them, creep them,
right up to your chin.
    (walk fingers up chest)
Open up your little mouth,
But do not let them in.
    (hide hands behind back)

Pancake

(*suit actions to words*)
Mix a pancake, stir a pancake,
Pop it in a pan.
Fry a pancake, toss a pancake,
Catch it if you can!

Patty Cake Patty Cake
(also known as *Pat-a-Cake*)

Patty cake, patty cake, baker's man,
Bake me a cake as fast as you can.
    (*clap hands*)
Roll it
    (*roll hands*)
and pat it
    (*clap hands*)
and mark it with a "B"
    (*draw letter "B" on child's hand, tummy or back*)
And there'll be enough for baby and me.
    (*clap hands*)

Pease Porridge Hot
(an easy bouncing rhyme or clapping game)

Pease porridge hot,
Pease porridge cold,
Pease porridge in the pot nine days old.
Some like it hot.
Some like it cold.
Some like it in the pot nine days old.

Plant a Little Seed
(Reprinted with permission, *Plant a Little Seed*, Stewart)

Plant a little seed
    (*one hand make cup/pot shape, other hand moves down
    through pot in time with the music*)
Watch it grow,
    (*plant hand comes back up through pot as if growing*)
Soon we will have a vegetable.
    (*one fist on top of other, then fist over fist "growing" upward*)

Note: At end of song hold up picture of vegetable or the real thing.
Ask what it might be, then name it.

Pop Goes the Weasel

A penny for a spool of thread,
A penny for a needle,
That's the way the money goes—
POP! goes the weasel.

Pussy Cat, Pussy Cat

Pussy cat, pussy cat, where have you been?
I've been to London to visit the queen.
Pussy cat, pussy cat, what did you there?
I frightened a little mouse under her chair.

Rain Is Falling Down

Rain is falling down, splash!
      (wiggle finger down in front of child or as tickle, making splashing motion at end of line)
Rain is falling down, splash!
Pitter patter pitter patter
Rain is falling down, SPLASH!
      (big splash at end; this is fun in the tub or pool)

Rain on the Green Grass

Rain on the green grass,
      (pound hands gently to make rain sounds for first three lines)
Rain on the tree.
Rain on the house top,
But not on me.
      (point to self and shake head "no" on last line)

Rain, Rain, Go Away

Rain, rain, go away,
Come again some other day.
Little [child's name] wants to play.
Rain, rain, go away.

Reach for the Ceiling

      (suit actions to words)
Reach for the ceiling,
Touch the floor,

Stand up again,
Let's do some more.
Touch your head,
Then your knee,
Up to your shoulders,
Like this, you see.
Reach for the ceiling,
Touch the floor.
That's all now,
There isn't anymore.

Ride a Cock Horse

Ride a cock horse
  (*bounce child on lap*)
To Banbury Cross,
To see a fine lady
Upon a white horse.
With rings on her fingers,
  (*tickle child's fingers*)
And bells on her toes,
  (*tickle child's toes*)
She shall have music,
Wherever she goes.
  (*bounce child on lap*)

Ride Baby Ride

Ride baby ride.
Ch, ch, ch, ch, ch, ch.
  (*bounce child on knee by raising the heel of your foot; can do*
   this at any pace and as long as child likes)
Ride that horsey ride.
Ch, ch, ch, ch, ch, ch. (repeat)
Whoa . . . .
  (*to end, say "Whoa" and give child a hug*)

Ring Around the Rosie

Ring around the rosie,
A pocket full of posies,
Ashes, ashes,
We all fall down!

Endings: if you want to get up again, try:

Pulling up the daisies,
Pulling up the daisies.
Hush-a, hush-a,
We all stand up.
>   *or*
Cows are in the meadow,
Eating buttercups.
Thunder, lightening,
>   (*gently pound hands on floor*)
We all stand up!
>   (*stand on last line*)

Roly-Poly

Roly-poly, roly-poly
up-up-up.
>   (*roll hands up*)
Roly-poly, roly-poly
out-out-out.
>   (*roll hands away from body*)
Roly-poly, roly-poly
clap-clap-clap.
>   (*clap*)
Roly-poly, roly-poly
Lay them in your lap!
>   (*put hands in lap*)

Rooster Crows

One, two, three,
>   (*bounce on knee*)
Baby's on my knee.
Rooster crows,
And away [child's name] goes!
>   (*lift child high in air or slide down legs*)

Round and Round the Garden

Round and round the garden goes the teddy bear.
>   (*trace circle on child's hand, back or tummy*)
One step, two step, tickle her/him under there.
>   (*move fingers up arm, tickle under chin or arm*)

Row, Row, Row Your Boat

> *(throughout, move hands and arms forward and backward in rowing motion; child may be on adult's lap or on floor between adult's legs, facing the adult or not)*

Row, row, row your boat,
Gently down the stream.
Merrily, merrily, merrily, merrily,
Life is but a dream.

Rub-a-Dub, Dub

Rub-a-dub dub,
Three men in a tub.
> *(rub belly with circular motion)*

And who do you think they be?
The butcher, the baker,
The candlestick maker.
> *(pat belly three times)*

Throw them out—
Knaves all three
> *(tickle)*

(Note: this rhyme can be adapted by changing the last two lines to "and [child's name] all went out to sea!")

Shoe the Old Horse

Shoe the old horse.
> *(pat child's foot)*

Shoe the old mare.
> *(pat child's other foot)*

Let the little pony run, bare, bare, bare.
> *(pat child's bottom)*

Sing a Song of Sixpence

Sing a song of sixpence,
A pocket full of rye.
Four and twenty blackbirds,
Baked in a pie.
When the pie was open,
The birds began to sing.
Wasn't that a dainty dish
To set before the king?

Snow Is Falling Down

(same actions as Rain Is Falling Down, except make shhhh motion with finger across lips)
Snow is falling down, shhhhh.
Snow is falling down, shhhhh.
Slowly, slowly, very slowly,
Snow is falling down, shhhhh.

Sometimes I Am Tall

Sometimes I am tall.
 (stand up straight)
Sometimes I am small.
 (bend or crouch to floor)
Sometimes I am very, very tall.
 (stand and stretch arms above head)
Sometimes I am very, very, small.
 (bend down toward floor)
Sometimes tall, sometimes small,
 (stretch high, bend low)
See how I am now!
 (stand up normally)

Star Light, Star Bright

Star light, star bright,
First star I see tonight,
I wish I may, I wish I might,
Have the wish I wish tonight.

Suppose

Do you suppose a giant
 (reach toward ceiling)
Who is tall—tall—tall,
Could ever be a brownie
Who is small—small—small?
 (crouch down on floor)
But the brownie who is tiny
Will try—try—try
To reach up to the giant
Who is high—high—high.
 (reach toward ceiling)

Teddy Bear, Teddy Bear

Teddy Bear, Teddy Bear turn around.
    (*turn body around*)
Teddy Bear, Teddy Bear touch the ground.
    (*lean down and touch floor*)
Teddy Bear, Teddy Bear show your shoe.
    (*wiggle foot*)
Teddy Bear, Teddy Bear that will do.
    (*clap on last three words*)
Teddy Bear, Teddy Bear go to bed.
    (*stretch as if yawning*)
Teddy Bear Teddy rest your head.
    (*rest head on hands*)
Teddy Bear, Teddy Bear turn out the light.
    (*cover eyes with hands*)
Teddy Bear, Teddy Bear say good night.
    (*wave goodbye*)

Ten Little Firemen

Ten little firemen sleeping in a row.
    (*hold child on lap*)
Ding-dong! Goes the bell,
    (*give child a gentle shake or tickle*)
Down the pole they go.
    (*run fingers down child's back or slide down adult's legs*)

There Was a Little Man

There was a little man
    (*point to child*)
He had a little crumb.
    (*tickle child's cheek*)
And over the mountain he did run.
    (*run fingers over child's head*)
With a belly full of fat,
    (*jiggle child's belly*)
And a big, tall hat,
    (*pat child's head*)
And a pancake stuck to his bun, bun, bun.
    (*pat child's bottom*)

These Are Grandma's Glasses

These are Grandma's glasses.
(*touch pointer finger and thumb together and for glasses around eyes*)
This is Grandma's hat.
(*point hands together above head*)
This is the way she folds her hands,
(*fold hands*)
And lays them in her lap.
(*put hands in lap*)

You can use other family member names as well.

This Is My Garden

This is my garden.
(*hold out one hand, palm up*)
I'll rake it with care.
(*use other hand to scratch palm*)
And then some flower seeds
I'll plant in there.
(*plant seeds on palm*)
The sun will shine,
(*arms above head in circle*)
The rain will fall.
(*wiggle fingers downward*)
And soon my garden
Will grow straight and tall.
(*stretch arms up slowly up above head*)

This Is the Way the Ladies Ride

This is the way the ladies ride prim, prim, prim.
(*bounce child gently on knee*)
This is the way the gentlemen ride trim, trim, trim.
(*bounce child slightly harder*)
This is the way the farmer rides trot, trot, trot.
(*bounce child by lifting first one knee then the other*)
This is the way the hunter rides a-gallop, a-gallop, a-gallop.
(*bounce child quickly*)

This Little Piggy

(*traditionally, wiggle each finger or toe per line, or you can*)

wiggle child's whole arm and leg, one for each line, ending with tickle on last line)
This little piggy went to market,
This little piggy stayed home.
This little piggy had roast beef,
And this little piggy had none.
And this little piggy ran wee, wee, wee, wee, wee,
All the way home.

Three Green and Speckled Frogs
(use the melody from *Little Songs for Little Me* by Stewart)

Three green and speckled frogs sat on a speckled log,
    (hold up three fingers)
Eating the most delicious bug, Yum, Yum!
    (rub tummy)
One jumped into the pool where it was nice and cool
    (hold up one finger)
Then there were two green speckled frogs, gulp, gulp!
    (hold up two fingers, repeat with two, one, to no frogs left)

Three Little Monkeys

Three little monkeys,
    (hold up three fingers)
Jumping on the bed.
    (jump fingers off palm of other hand)
One fell off and bumped his head.
    (pat head gently)
Mama called the doctor
    (hold one hand to ear as if on phone)
and the doctor said,
Put those monkeys right to bed.
    (shake pointer finger)

To Market, to Market

    (bounce child up and down on knee throughout)
To market, to market, to buy a fat pig,
Home again, home again, jiggity jig.
To market, to market, to buy a fat hog,
Home again, home again, jiggity jog.

Tommy Thumbs Up

(*using thumbs, follow actions*)
Tommy Thumbs up and Tommy Thumbs down,
Tommy Thumbs dancing all around the town.
Dance them on your shoulders,
Dance them on your head.
Dance them on your knees and
Tuck them into bed.
(*make fists on last line*)

Trot, Trot to Boston

(*child sits facing adult on lap, bounce to rhyme*)
Trot, trot to Boston,
Trot, trot to Lynn,
Look out [child's name]
You're going to fall in!
(*open legs and while holding firmly let the child slip through opening*)

Twinkle, Twinkle Little Star

Twinkle, twinkle little star,
(*hands in air and wiggle fingers*)
How I wonder what you are,
(*scratch head or pointer finger against cheek*)
Up above the world so high,
Like a diamond in the sky.
(*wave hands above head*)
Twinkle, twinkle little star,
How I wonder what you are.
(*hands in air and wiggle fingers*)

Two Little Blackbirds
(see also Dos Pajaritos)

Two little blackbirds sitting on a hill.
(*hold both hands up in air*)
One named Jack, the other named Jill.
(*hold up one hand, then the other*)
Fly away Jack, fly away Jill.
(*move hands behind back*)
Come back Jack, come back Jill.
(*bring hands back into the front of body*)

You can change the color of the birds, if desired.

Warm Hands Warm

Warm hands, warm,
Do you know how?
If you want to warm your hands,
     (*rub hands together while saying above lines*)
Blow on them now.
     (*blow gently on your hands*)

Wash the Dishes

Wash the dishes,
Wipe the dishes,
     (*wipe hands down child's arms on first two lines*)
Ring the bell for tea.
     (*touch nose for bell*)
Three good wishes,
three good kisses,
     (*wipe hands down child's arms on "wishes" and "kisses"*)
I will give to thee.
     (*kiss on "thee"*)

Way Up High in the Apple Tree

Way up high in the apple tree
     (*hold arms above head*)
Two little apples did I see.
     (*make two fists*)
So I shook that tree as hard as I could
     (*shake and wiggle body*)
An d-o-w-n came the apples.
     (*lower arms*)
Umm! They were good!
     (*rub tummy*)

Wheels on the Bus

The wheels on the bus go round and round,
round and round, round and round.
The wheels on the bus, go round and round,
All through the town.
     (*roll hands together*)
The windows on the bus go up and down, . . .
     (*lift arms up and down*)
The doors on the bus go open and shut, . . .

(*clap hands together*)
The horn of the bus goes beep, beep, beep, . . .
    (*tap child's nose or pat belly*)
The wipers on the bus go swish, swish, swish, . . .
    (*wave hands back and forth in front of body*)
The wheels on the bus go round and round, . . .
    (*roll hands together*)

When Ducks Get Up in the Morning
(Reprinted with permission, *Plant a Little Seed,* by Stewart.)

    (*slap thighs in rhythm or clap to keep rhythm; you can also
        hold up a picture of an animal or a stuffed animal*)
When ducks get up in the morning, they always say good day.
When ducks get up in the morning, they always say good day.
Quack, quack, quack, quack, that is what they say, they say
Quack, quack, quack, quack, that is what they say.

Repeat, using other animals.

Where Is Thumbkin?

Where is Thumbkin? Where is Thumbkin?
    (*hands behind back*)
"Here I am, here I am."
    (*hold up one thumb, then the other*)
"How are you today, Sir?"
"Very well, I thank you."
Run away, run away.
    (*hide hands behind back or just make fists*)
Where is Pointer? Where is Pointer?
"Here I am, here I am."
    (*hold up pointer/index finger on one hand, then the other*)
"How are you today, Sir?"
"Very well, I thank you."
Run away, run away.
    (*hide hands behind back or just make fists*)

Whoops, Johnny!

Johnny, Johnny, Johnny, Johnny,
    (*start at little finger, tapping each one in turn*)
Whoops, Johnny.
    (*on Whoops slide down index finger and up thumb, tap thumb*)

Whoops, Johnny, Johnny, Johnny, Johnny.
> (*slide down thumb and up index finger, tap index*)

You can use child's name.

Wiggle Your Fingers

> (*wiggle appropriate body part*)

Wiggle your fingers.
Wiggle your toes.
Wiggle your shoulders.
Now, wiggle your nose.

Zoom Down the Freeway

> (*this action rhyme is best done with adult sitting on the floor with legs out straight in front, with child sitting on knees of adult*)

Zoom down the freeway,
Zoom down the freeway,
Zoom down the freeway,
> (*slide arms forward on "zoom"*)

FAST!
> (*clap hands on "fast"*)

Up goes the drawbridge,
Up goes the drawbridge,
Up goes the drawbridge,
> (*raise knees so child goes up*)

A ship is going past.
Down goes the drawbridge,
Down goes the drawbridge,
Down goes the drawbridge,
> (*lower knees so child goes down*)

The ship has passed at last.
Zoom down the freeway,
Zoom down the freeway,
Zoom down the freeway,
> (*slide arms forward on "zoom"*)

FAST!
> (*clap hands on "fast"*)

Resources for Nursery Rhymes, Fingerplays, and Songs

Briggs, Diane. *101 Fingerplays, Stories and Songs to Use with Finger Puppets.* Chicago: American Library Association, 1999.

Chorao, Kay. *Knock at the Door and Other Baby Action Rhymes.*
New York: Dutton, 1999.
Very simple, with one rhyme and illustrations on each connecting
two-page spread. Includes illustrated and written directions for
rhymes. This can be used during the story time.

Davis, Sandra Carpenter. *Bounce Me Tickle Me Hug Me: Lap Rhymes
and Play Rhymes from Around the World.* Toronto: The Parent-
Child Mother Goose Program, 1997.
Rhymes are printed in the original language of the rhyme, with English translations and directions.

Defty, Jeff. *Creative Fingerplays and Action Rhymes: An Index and
Guide to Their Use.* Phoenix, Ariz.: Oryx, 1992.
Text provides action verses for infants through older children, ESL
and special needs children, a subject index, and first-line index. Also
a section on evaluating, selecting, and teaching action verses.

Dunn, Opal. *Hippety-Hop Hippety Hay: Growing with Rhymes from
Birth to Age Three.* New York: Henry Holt, 1999.
One to two rhymes per page, with directions for action under the
rhyme/poem. Music scores included in separate chapter.

Flint Public Library. *Ring a Ring O' Roses: Stories, Games and Finger
Plays for Pre-School Children.* 10th ed. Flint, Mich.: Flint Public
Library, 1996.
The 10th edition of this collection of fingerplays for preschool children is arranged by subject and does include a first-line index for
easy access. Does include Spanish translations of familiar English
fingerplays along with traditional Spanish fingerplays.

Griego, Marot, Betsy Bucks, Sharon Gilbert ,and Laurel Kimball, trans.
Tortillitas para Mama and Other Nursery Rhymes. New York: Holt,
Rinehart and Winston, 1981.
Has rhymes in Spanish and English.

Jaeger, Sally. *From Wibbleton to Wobbleton.* Produced by 49 North
Production, Inc. Dist. by Instructional Video. 40 mins. 1998, 1999
release. ISBN 0968450806. Videocassette and booklet.

Kleiner, Lynn. *Babies Make Music.* Produced and directed by Lynn
Kleiner and Dennis Devine. 52 mins. Music Rhapsody, 1996. ISBN
0965363619. Videocassette.

Orozco, Jose-Luis. *Diez Deditos: Ten Little Fingers and Other Play
Rhymes and Action Songs form Latin America.* New York: Dutton,
1997.
Spanish action rhymes and songs, including English translations.
This has both written and illustrated instructions.

Ra, Carol R. *Trot Trot to Boston: Play Rhymes for Baby.* New York:
Lothrop, Lee and Shepard, 1987.

Scott, Anne. *The Laughing Baby: Remembering Nursery Rhymes and*

Reasons. Songs and Rhymes from Around the World. South Hadley, Mass.: Bergin and Garvey, 1987.
Songs and rhymes from around the world. This text includes music for the rhymes and songs, the origin of the rhyme and the directions on how to do the action.
Sierra, Judy. *The Flannel Board Storytelling Book.* 2nd ed. New York: H. W. Wilson, 1997.
Stewart, Nancy. *Plant a Little Seed: Songs for Growing Children* from Friends Street Music, 1995.

SAMPLE THEME AND GRAB-BAG PROGRAMS
Opening and Closing the Program

It is recommended that each program begin and/or end each time with the same material. You do not have to use the same material at both times, but the very young child will respond to something familiar. I use "If You're Happy and You Know It" as both an opening and a closing song. You might prefer beginning with a stretch and ending with "Ring Around the Rosy" as another option. Stretches are also a good way to get wiggles out and settle the children and adults into the program. Some stretch rhymes include: Way Up High in the Apple Tree, Sometimes I Am Tall, Suppose, Bend and Stretch, The Grand Old Duke of York, Reach for the Ceiling, and Head and Shoulders, Knees and Toes. Simply adding a verse such as "If you're happy and you know it, wave bye-bye!" can make for a closing song. Find what you feel comfortable with, and make it yours!

Theme Programs

The following material has been arranged by themes. Each theme consists of stories, rhymes, fingerplays, and songs that can be incorporated into the program. If the material can be used by more than one theme, it is indicated in the heading. Keep in mind the brevity of this type of program, and select the material you feel most comfortable with.

The majority of rhymes, fingerplays, and songs are of European origin and are in English. For more multiethnic selections, look to the resources in the rhymes, fingerplays, and songs section or consult chapter 5. The material offered here can be used as a starting place for you to create your own unique program whether you use a theme or not.

Bear in mind that not all of the stories, rhymes, fingerplays, and songs previously listed have been used in the following theme program listing. Some of them can be found in a collection of *Mother Goose.* All of them do, however, work well with the very young child.

ANIMALS—FARMS/FARMS
Stories

The ABC Bunny, by Wanda Gag
Across the Stream, by Mirra Ginsburg
And So Can I! by Bill Gillham
Animal Moves, by Dawn Apperley
Animal Noises, by Dawn Apperley
Are You My Daddy? by Carla Dijs
Are You My Mommy? by Carla Dijs
As Quiet as a Mouse, by Hilda Offen
Ask Mr. Bear, by Marjorie Flack
Barnyard Banter, by Denise Fleming
Blink Like an Owl, by Kate Burns
The Box with Red Wheels, by Maud and Miska Petersham
Brown Bear, Brown Bear, by Bill Martin
The Chick and the Duckling, by V. Suteyev
Come Out, Muskrats, by Jim Arnosky
Ducks Fly, by Lydia Dabcovich
From Head to Toe, by Eric Carle
The Golden Egg Book, by Margaret Brown
Good Night, Good Night, by Sandra Boynton
Honk! by Chris Demarest
I Love Animals, by Flora McDonnell
In the Small, Small Pond, by Denise Fleming
In the Tall, Tall Grass, by Denise Fleming
Is That an Elephant Over There? by Rebecca Elgar
Little Bird, by Saviour Pirotta
Little Gorilla, by Ruth Bornstein
My Barn, by Craig Brown
Oh, A-Hunting We Will Go, by John Langstaff
Old MacDonald Had a Farm, by Frances Cony
One Red Rooster, by Kathleen Carroll
Over in the Meadow, by John Langstaff
The Owl and the Pussycat, by Edward Lear
Peek a Moo! by Marie Cimarusti
Runaway Rabbit, by Ron Maris
Sam Who Never Forgets, by Eve Rice
Says Who? by David Carter
Tail Toes Eyes Ears Nose, by Marilee Burton
This Is the Farmer, by Nancy Tafuri
Toddlerobics Animal Fun, by Zita Newcome
Waddle Like a Duck, by Kate Burns
Who Said Meow? by Marie Polushkin

Rhymes, Fingerplays, and Songs

Baa, Baa, Black Sheep
Gray Squirrel
Here Is a Bunny
Little Boy Blue, Come Blow Your Horn
Little Turtle
Mary Had a Little Lamb
Mr. Turkey and Mr. Duck
Old MacDonald Had a Farm
Plant a Little Seed
Rooster Crows
Shoe the Old Horse
This Is the Way the Ladies Ride
This Little Pig had a Scrub-a-Dub Dub (from *The Baby Record*)
This Little Piggy
Three Little Ducks Went Out One Day, by Raffi
To Market, to Market
Two Little Blackbirds
Way Up High in the Apple Tree
When Ducks Get Up in the Morning

ANIMALS—JUNGLE/ELEPHANTS/ZOO
Stories

Are You My Daddy? by Carla Dijs
Dads Are Such Fun, by Jakki Wood
Is That an Elephant Over There? by Rebecca Elgar
Little Elephant, by Miela Ford and Tana Hoban
Little Gorilla, by Ruth Bornstein
Sam Who Never Forgets, by Eve Rice
Splash!, by Flora McDonnell

Rhymes, Fingerplays, and Songs

Bingo
An Elephant Goes Like This and That, Joanna Cole
Gray Squirrel
Here Comes a Mouse
Here Is a Bunny
Here Is a Nest for a Robin, Flint Public Library
Hickory Dickory Dock
Leg over Leg
Mama's Taking Us to the Zoo Tomorrow, by Raffi
Pussy Cat, Pussy Cat
This Little Piggy
Three Little Monkeys
Two Little Blackbirds

BABIES: see FAMILIES

BATHTIME/WATER
Stories
Across the Stream, by Mirra Ginsburg
Blue Sea, by Robert Kalan
Come Out, Muskrats, by Jim Arnosky
Have You Seen My Duckling? by Nancy Tafuri
I Love Boats, by Flora McDonnell
In the Small, Small Pond, by Denise Fleming
Little Elephant, by Miela Ford and Tana Hoban
My Blue Boat, by Chris Demarest
Splash! by Flora McDonnell
Tom and Pippo Go for a Walk, by Helen Oxenbury

Rhymes, Fingerplays, and Songs
Catch Me and Kiss Me and Say It Again, by Clyde Watson
Charlie Over the Water, by Tom Glazer
Fishies
Gack-Goon
The Great Big Spider
I'm a Little Teapot
Jack and Jill Went Up the Hill
Little Turtle
1,2,3,4,5, I Caught a Fish Alive, by Iona and Peter Opie
Rain Is Falling Down
Rain, Rain Go Away
Row, Row, Row Your Boat
Rub-a-Dub, Dub
This Is the Way We Wash Our Face
Three Green and Speckled Frogs

BEARS
Stories
Ask Mr. Bear, by Marjorie Flack
Bears, by Ruth Krauss
How Do I Put It On? by Shigeo Wantanabe
Just Like Daddy, by Frank Asch
The Little Mouse, the Red Ripe Strawberry and the Big Hungry Bear,
    by Don and Audrey Wood
Panda Big and Panda Small, by Jane Cabrera
Sleepy Bear, by Lydia Dabcovich
Where Is Alice's Bear? by Fiona Pragoff

Rhymes, Fingerplays, and Songs

The Bear Went Over the Mountain
Going on a Bear Hunt
Round and Round the Garden
Teddy Bear, Teddy Bear

BEDTIME
Stories

Busy Lizzie, by Holly Berry
Good Night, Good Night, by Sandra Boynton
Goodnight Moon, by Margaret Wise Brown
Grandfather Twilight, by Barbara Berger
I Hear, by Rachel Isadora
Piggies, by Don and Audrey Wood
Ten, Nine, Eight, by Molly Bang
Time for Bed, by Mem Fox

Rhymes, Fingerplays, and Songs

Baby's Nap
Jack Be Nimble
Star Light, Star Bright
Teddy Bear, Teddy Bear
There Were Five in the Bed
Three Little Monkeys
Twinkle Twinkle, Little Star

BIRDS
Stories

The Big Fat Worm, by Nancy Van Laan
Little Bird, Saviour Pirotta
Little Robin Redbreast, by Shari Halpern
Owl and the Pussycat, by Edward Lear

Rhymes, Fingerplays, and Songs

Dos Pajaritos
Here Is a Nest for a Robin
Hickety, Pickety My Black Hen
Little White Duck, by Burl Ives
Mr. Turkey and Mr. Duck
One, Two, Buckle My Shoe
Rooster Crows
Sing a Song of Sixpence
Tall as a Tree
Three Little Ducks Went Out One Day, by Raffi
Two Little Blackbirds
Way Up High in the Apple Tree

BIRTHDAYS/ GROWING UP
Stories

Ask Mr. Bear, by Marjorie Flack
Benny Bakes a Cake, by Eve Rice
Little Gorilla, by Ruth Bornstein

Rhymes, Fingerplays, and Songs

Do You Know the Muffin Man?
Happy Birthday to You
Head and Shoulders, Knees and Toes
Here's a Cup
I'm a Little Teapot
If You're Happy and You Know It
Pancake
Patty Cake
Pease Porridge Hot
Sometimes I Am Tall
Suppose
Tall as a Tree
These Are [child's name] Fingers, by Bob McGrath

BOATS: see THINGS THAT GO

BUGS: see GARDENS

CATS/DOGS
Stories

Along Came Toto, by Ann Axworthy
Benny Bakes a Cake, by Eve Rice
The Big Fat Worm, by Nancy Van Laan
Hunky Dory Ate It! by Katie Evans
Hunky Dory Found It! by Katie Evans
Where's Spot? by Eric Hill
Who Said Meow? by Marie Polushkin

Rhymes, Fingerplays, and Songs

Bingo
Here Comes a Mouse
Hey Diddle, Diddle
Hickory Dickory Dock
How Much Is That Doggie in the Window?
Leg over Leg
Pussy Cat Pussy Cat

CHICKENS/DUCKS
Stories

Across the Stream, by Mirra Ginsburg
The Chick and the Duckling, by V. Suteyev
Come Along Daisy, by Jane Simmons
Ducks Fly, by Lydia Dabcovich
Five Little Ducks, by Ian Beck
Five Little Ducks, by Raffi
The Golden Egg Book, by Margaret Wise Brown
Have You Seen My Duckling? by Nancy Tafuri

Rhymes, Fingerplays, and Songs

Five Little Ducks Went Out One Day
Hickety Pickety, My Black Hen
Mr. Turkey and Mr. Duck
One, Two, Buckle My Shoe
When Ducks Get Up in the Morning

CLOUDS: see WEATHER

DOGS: see CATS/DOGS

DUCKS: see CHICKENS/DUCKS

ELEPHANTS: see ANIMALS—JUNGLE

FAMILIES/BABIES/MOTHERS/FATHERS
Stories

Are You My Daddy? by Carla Dijs
Are You My Mommy? by Carla Dijs
Ask Mr. Bear, by Marjorie Flack
Baby in the Box, by Frank Asch
Baby Loves, by Michael Lawrence
The Box with Red Wheels, by Maud and Miska Petersham
Clap Hands, by Helen Oxenbury
Come Along Daisy! by Jane Simmons
Dads Are Such Fun, by Jakki Wood
Have You Seen My Duckling? by Nancy Tafuri
Honk! by Chris Demarest
I See, by Rachel Isadora
Just Like Daddy, by Frank Asch
"More, More, More," Said the Baby, by Sue Williams
On Mother's Lap, by Ann Scott
Pots and Pans, by Patricia Hubbel

The Saucepan Game, by Jan Omerod
Tickle, Tickle, by Helen Oxenbury
When You Were a Baby, by Ann Jonas
Whose Mouse Are You? by Robert Kraus

Rhymes, Fingerplays, and Songs
Come'a Look'a See, Here's My Mama, by Bob McGrath
Here Are Grandma's Glasses
Mother and Father and Uncle John
Patty Cake
There Was a Little Man
These Are [child's name] Fingers
This Is My Father, This Is My Mother
Tommy Thumbs Up, by Bob McGrath
Where Is Grandma? Where Is Grandma?, by Bernice Harris

FARMS: see ANIMALS—FARMS

FATHERS: see FAMILIES

FOOD/MESSES
Stories
Hunky Dory Ate It! by Katie Evans
The Little Mouse, the Red Ripe Strawberry and the Big Hungry Bear,
   by Don and Audrey Wood
Lunch, by Denise Fleming
Oh No, Anna! by Vivian French
Pots and Pans, by Patricia Hubbel
Sam Who Never Forgets, by Eve Rice
What's for Lunch? by Eric Carle

Rhymes, Fingerplays, and Songs
Acka Backa
Criss, Cross, Applesauce
Cup of Tea, Flint Public Library
Do You Know the Muffin Man?
Five Fat Peas in a Pea-pod Pressed, by Lois Sharon
Georgie Porgie
Hot Cross Buns
Humpty Dumpty
I'm a Little Teapot
Pancake
Patty Cake, Patty Cake
Pease Porridge Hot

Sing a Song of Sixpence
There Was a Little Man
To Market to Market
Tortillas Tortillas, Flint Public Library
Wash the Dishes
Way Up High in The Apple Tree

GAMES: see TOYS

GARDENS/BUGS/OUTSIDE
Stories

The Big Fat Worm, by Nancy Van Laan
Bug Hunt, by Neecy Twinem
The Carrot Seed, by Ruth Krauss
I Went Walking, by Sue Williams
In My Garden, by Ron Maris
In the Small, Small Pond, by Denise Fleming
In the Tall, Tall Grass, by Denise Fleming
Titch, by Pat Hutchins
Tom and Pippo Go for a Walk, by Helen Oxenbury
Tom and Pippo in the Snow, by Helen Oxenbury

Rhymes, Fingerplays, and Songs
All Around the Mulberry Bush
Arabella Miller
Five Fat Peas in a Pea-pod Pressed
Gack-Goon
Gray Squirrel
The Great Big Spider
Here Is the Beehive
Little Turtle
Mary, Mary Quite Contrary
Plant a Little Seed
Round and Round the Garden
Slowly, Slowly Very Slowly Creeps the Garden Snail, on *Baby Record*
Tall as a Tree
This Is My Garden
Three Green and Speckled Frogs
Way Up High in the Apple Tree

GETTING DRESSED/HATS
Stories

A Fox Got My Socks, by Hilda Offen
Benny's Four Hats, by Ruth Jaynes

How Do I Put It On? by Shigeo Wantanabe
Look, There's My Hat! by Maureen Roffey
Whose Hat? by Margaret Miller

Rhymes, Fingerplays, and Songs
All Around the Cobbler's Bench [Mulberry Bush]
Cobbler, Cobbler
Head and Shoulders, Knees and Toes
Here Are [child's name] Fingers
If You're Wearing [color] Today
Mitten Weather, in *Ring A Ring O-Rosie*
Shoe the Old Horse
These Are Grandma's Glasses
Tommy Thumbs Up
Warm Hands Warm.

HATS: see GETTING DRESSED

MESSES: see FOOD

MICE
Stories
Lunch, by Denise Fleming
The Little Mouse, the Red Ripe Strawberry and the Big Hungry Bear,
    by Don and Audrey Wood
Noisy Nora, by Rosemary Wells
This Is the Farmer, by Nancy Tafuri
Whose Mouse Are You? by Robert Kraus

Rhymes, Fingerplays, and Songs
Here Comes a Mouse
Hickory, Dickory Dock
Pussy Cat, Pussy Cat
Slowly Slowly Very Slowly on *Baby Record*
Wiggle Your Fingers

MONKEYS
Stories
Tom and Pippo Go for a Walk, by Helen Oxenbury
Tom and Pippo in the Snow, by Helen Oxenbury
What's for Lunch? by Eric Carle

Rhymes, Fingerplays, and Songs
All Around the Mulberry Bush

Three Little Monkeys
Wiggle Your Fingers

MOTHERS: see FAMILIES

OUTSIDE: see GARDENS

PLAY: see TOYS

PIGS
Stories

Do Pigs Have Stripes? by Melanie Walsh
I Like Me! by Nancy Carlson
Piggies, by Don and Audrey Wood

Rhymes, Fingerplay, and Songs
This Little Pig Had a Scrub-a-Dub, on *Baby Record*
This Little Piggy Went to Market
To Market to Market

RABBITS
Stories

The ABC Bunny, by Wanda Gag
The Golden Egg Book, by Margaret Wise Brown
Goodnight Moon, by Margaret Wise Brown
Home for a Bunny, by Margaret Wise Brown
The Runaway Rabbit, by Ron Maris
What Can Rabbit See? by Lucy Cousins

Rhymes, Fingerplays, and Songs
Here Is a Nest for a Robin
Here's a Bunny with Ears so Funny
Wiggle Your Fingers

RAIN: see WEATHER

SEASONS: see WEATHER

SHEEP
Stories

Mary Had a Little Lamb, by Sarah Hale
Sheep in a Jeep, by Nancy Shaw

Rhymes, Fingerplays, and Songs

Baa, Baa, Black Sheep
Little Boy Blue
Mary Had a Little Lamb

THINGS THAT GO/BOATS/TRAINS
Stories

Chugga-Chugga Choo-Choo, by Kevin Lewis
Freight Train, by Donald Crews
I Love Boats, by Flora McDonnell
My Blue Boat, by Chris Demarest
Sheep in a Jeep, by Nancy Shaw
Trucks and Other Working Wheels, by Jan Pienkowski

Rhymes, Fingerplays, and Songs

Airplanes Fly in the Sky
Dance to Your Daddy
Down by the Station
The Engine
Five Little Boats, by Judy Sierra
The Grand Old Duke of York
Here Is a Choo Choo Train
Here Is the Engine
I'll Drive a Dump Truck
Lots of Cars
Row, Row, Row Your Boat
This Is the Way the Ladies Ride
Trot Trot to Boston
Wheels on the Bus
Zoom Down the Freeway

TOYS/PLAY/GAMES
Stories

Baby in the Box, by Frank Asch
The Ball Bounced, by Nancy Tafuri
Bounce, Bounce, Bounce, by Kathy Henderson
Bouncing, by Shirley Hughes
Busy Lizzie., by Holly Berry
Chugga-Chugga Choo-Choo, by Kevin Lewis
Clap Your Hands, by Lorinda Cauley
Hunky Dory Found It! by Katie Evans
Is That an Elephant Over There? by Rebecca Elgar
Just Like Jasper! by Nick Butterworth
Now We Can Go, by Ann Jonas

Peek-a-Boo, by Matthew Price
Peek a Moo! by Marie Cimarusti
Piggies, by Don and Audrey Wood
Pots and Pans, by Patricia Hubbel
The Saucepan Game, by Jan Omerod
Says Who? by David Carter
Tail Toes Eyes Ears Nose, by Marilee Burton
Tickle, Tickle, by Helen Oxenbury
Titch, by Pat Hutchins
Tom and Pippo Go for a Walk, by Helen Oxenbury
Tom and Pippo in the Snow, by Helen Oxenbury
Where Is Alice's Bear? by Fiona Pragoff

Rhymes, Fingerplays, and Songs
All Around the Mulberry Bush
All for Baby
Bumping Up and Down, by Raffi
Drums
Here Comes a Mouse
Here's a Ball
Here We Go Up, Up, Up
Hickory, Dickory Dock
Humpty Dumpty
Jack Be Nimble
Jack in the Box
Johnny Hammers One Hammer
Let Everyone Clap Hands Like Me, by Tom Glazer
Little Turtle
Ring Around the Rosie
See My Pony, My Jet Black Pony
Teddy Bear, Teddy Bear
This Is the Way the Ladies Ride
Three Little Monkeys
Two Little Blackbirds
Wiggle Your Fingers

TRAINS: see THINGS THAT GO

WATER: see BATHTIME

WEATHER/RAIN/CLOUDS/SEASONS
Stories
The Five Little Pumpkins, by Iris Van Rynbach
In the Small, Small Pond, by Denise Fleming

The Little Cloud, by Eric Carle
Rain, by Robert Kalan
Sleepy Bear, by Lydia Dabcovich
Tom and Pippo in the Snow, by Helen Oxenbury
Who Is Tapping at My Window? by A. G. Deming

Rhymes, Fingerplays, and Songs

Dr. Foster
The Great Big Spider
I Hear Thunder
It's Raining, It's Pouring
Rain Is Falling Down
Rain on the Green Grass
Rain, Rain, Go Away
Snow Is Falling Down
Mitten Weather, Flint Public Library
Warm Hands Warm
Wheels on the Bus

Grab-Bag Programs

The following are actual program outlines that are not necessarily theme related. They can be used verbatim or adapted to your own style. The group's dynamics will also determine what material you actually use. With active groups, more rhymes, songs, and other active literary experiences are much more beneficial than trying to use all the books suggested. If a title for this type of program is important to you, pick a general one that will leave you lots of room for program flexibility—something like "Grab-Bag Stories," "Story Stew," "Mother Goose on the Loose." The ones presented here are given in no particular order or value and run about twenty to thirty minutes.

Program 1

Opening: stretch with Sometimes I Am Tall
Rhyme: Open, Shut Them
Rhyme: Teddy Bear, Teddy Bear
Story: *Brown Bear, Brown Bear*, by Bill Martin
Song: Wheels on the Bus
Rhyme: Here's a Ball
Fingerplay: These Are [child's name] Fingers
Rhyme: Way Up High in the Apple Tree
Rhyme: Jack in the Box
Story: *I Hear*, by Rachel Isadora
Closing: The More We Get Together

Program 2

Opening Song: The More We Get Together
Rhyme: Patty Cake
Rhyme: Hickory, Dickory Dock
Song: Row, Row, Row Your Boat
Book: *Brown Bear, Brown Bear,* by Bill Martin
Rhyme: Teddy Bear, Teddy Bear Turn Around
Song: The Bear Went over the Mountain
Rhyme: Open, Shut Them
Tickle: Round and Round the Garden
Book: *Barnyard Tracks,* by Dee Dee Duffy
Rhyme: Two Little Blackbirds (use flannel-board pieces)
Fingerplay/Song: Mr. Turkey and Mr. Duck
Closing Song: The More We Get Together

Program 3

Opening Rhyme: Open, Shut Them
Rhyme: Patty Cake
Fingerplay: Hickory, Dickory Dock
Book: *Is That an Elephant Over There?* By Rebecca Elgar
Rhyme: An Elephant Goes Like This and That
Song: Three Little Monkeys
Book: *Sam Who Never Forgets,* by Eve Rice
Rhyme: Humpty Dumpty
Song: Old MacDonald Had a Farm (use flannel-board)
Book: *Piggies,* by Don and Audrey Wood
Closing Song: The More We Get Together

Program 4

Opening Song: The More We Get Together
Knee Bounce: Mother and Father and Uncle John
Book: *Benny's Four Hats,* by Ruth Jaynes
Lap Game or Standing: Here We Go Up, Up, Up
Stretch: Rain Is Falling Down
Book: *And So Can I!* by Bill Gillham
Lap Game: Leg over Leg
Book: *Brown Bear, Brown Bear,* by Bill Martin
Song: The Wheels on the Bus
Fingerplay: Three Little Monkeys
Closing: play Ring Around the Rosie

Program 5

Opening Song: The More We Get Together
Fingerplay: Fast Slow Song, by Nancy Stewart

Book: *If You're Happy and You Know It Clap Your Hands,* by David Carter
Lap Game or Standing: Here We Go Up, Up, Up
Stretch: Jack in the Box
Rhyme: Cobbler, Cobbler
Book: *Do Pigs Have Stripes?* by Melanie Walsh
Tickle: Criss Cross Applesauce
Book: *The Saucepan Game,* by Jan Ormerod (use pot prop)
Flannelboard or Puppet: Two Little Blackbirds
Closing song: The More We Get Together

Program 6

Opening Song: The More We Get Together
Fingerplay: Rain Is Falling Down
Book: *Blue Sea,* by Robert Kalan
Rhyme: 1-2-3-4-5, I Caught a Fish Alive
Lap Game: Leg over Leg
Book: *Are You My Mommy?* by Carla Dijs
Fingerpuppets: Two Little Blackbirds (flannel-board pieces)
Bounce: My Pony Macaroni
Lap Game or Standing: Hickory, Dickory Dock
Song: I Hear Thunder
Book: *Along Came Toto,* by Ann Axworthy
Tickle: Criss Cross Applesauce
Rhyme/Bounce: Humpty Dumpty
Closing Song: The More We Get Together

Program 7

Opening Song: The More We Get Together
Fingerplay: Open, Shut Them
Lap Game: Head and Shoulders, Knees and Toes
Book: *The Carrot Seed,* by Ruth Krauss (book can be used as is, as flannel-board story, or in its big-book format)
Fingerplay: Way Up High in the Apple Tree
Rhyme/Song: The Great Big Spider
Rhyme: Tall as a Tree (see Ernst, 1995)
Book: *The Little Mouse, the Red Ripe Strawberry and the Big Hungry Bear,* by Don and Audrey Wood
Song: The Wheels on the Bus
Bounce: Humpty Dumpty
Rhyme: Round and Round the Garden
Book: *Where's Spot?* by Eric Hill
Fingerplay: Tommy Thumbs Up
Bounce: Bump'n Downtown in My Little Red Wagon

Closing Song: If You're Happy and You Know It

Program 8

Opening Song: The More We Get Together
Fingerplay: Open, Shut Them
Fingerplay: Roly Poly
Action Song: Head and Shoulders, Knees and Toes
Book: *The Big Fat Worm,* by Nancy Van Laan
Fingerplay: There Was a Little Man
Song/Game: Mr. Turkey and Mr. Duck
Tickle: Round and Round the Garden
Fingerplay: 1-2-3-4-5, I Caught a Fish Alive
Book: *What Can Rabbit See?* by Lucy Cousins
Song: Row, Row, Row Your Boat
Rhyme/Game: Here Is My Garden
Book: *Titch,* by Pat Hutchins
Song: Plant a Little Seed (use visuals)
Fingerplay: Five Plump Peas
Closing Song: The More We Get Together

Program 9

Opening Song: The More We Get Together
Fingerplay: Head and Shoulders, Knees and Toes
Fingerplay: Tommy Thumbs Up
Book: *Brown Bear, Brown Bear,* by Bill Martin
Song: Row, Row, Row Your Boat
Rhyme: Hickory, Dickory Dock
Song: Old MacDonald Had a Farm (use stuffed toys pulled from cloth bag)
Rhyme/Game: The Great Big Spider
Rhyme: Tall as a Tree (do standing)
Rhyme: Jack in the Box
Book: *Mary Had a Little Lamb,* by Sarah Hale
Tickle: Round and Round the Garden
Rhyme: Here Is a Bunny
Bounce: This Is the Way the Ladies Ride
Tickle: Criss Cross Applesauce
Closing Song: The More We Get Together

Program 10

Opening: stretch with Suppose
Rhyme: Wiggle Your Fingers
Song: Bump'n Downtown in My Little Red Wagon
Rhyme: 1-2-3-4-5, I Caught a Fish Alive

Book: *Brown Bear, Brown Bear,* by Bill Martin
Bounce: To Market, to Market
Song: Wheels on the Bus
Tickle: Here Comes a Mouse (use a mouse puppet)
Rhyme: Tall as a Tree
Rhyme: Jack in the Box
Story: *Just Like Jasper!,* by Nick Butterworth
Rhyme: Humpty Dumpty
Rhyme/Song: The Great Big Spider
Rhyme: Cobbler, Cobbler
Book: *I Hear,* by Rachel Isadora
Closing Song: The More We Get Together

RESOURCES FOR PROGRAMMING IDEAS

BOOKS

Cobb, Jane. *I'm a Little Teapot! Presenting Preschool Storytime.* Vancouver, Brit. Col.: Black Sheep Press, 1996.

Ernst, Linda L. *Lapsit Services for the Very Young: A How-to-Do-It Manual.* New York: Neal-Schuman, 1995.

Feinberg, Sandra, and Kathleen Deerr. *Running a Parent/Child Workshop: A How-to-Do-It Manual for Librarians.* New York: Neal-Schuman, 1995.

Jeffery, Debby Ann. *Literate Beginnings: Programs for Babies and Toddlers.* Chicago: American Library Association, 1995.

Marino, Jane, and Dorothy F. Houlihan. *Mother Goose Time: Library Programs for Babies and Their Caregivers.* New York: Wilson, 1992.

Nespeca, Sue McCleaf. *Library Programming for Families with Young Children: A How-to-Do-It Manual.* New York: Neal-Schuman, 1994.

Nichols, Judy. *Storytimes for Two-Year-Olds.* 2d ed. Chicago: American Library Association, 1998.

ARTICLES:

Dowd, Frances Smardo, and Judith Dixon. "Successful Toddler Storytimes Based on Child Development Principles." *Public Libraries* (November/December 1996): 374–80.

Feldman, Sari, and Robert Needleman. "Take Two Board Books, and Call Me in the Morning." *School Library Journal* (June 1999): 30.

Hardman, Margaret, and Lynn Jones. "Sharing Books with Babies: Evaluation of an Early Literacy Intervention." *Educational Review* (November 1999): 221–29.

Knoth, Maeve Visser. "Reading Aloud to Very Young Children." *Book Links* (July 1998): 22–24.

Kupetz, Barbara N. "A Shared Responsibility: Nurturing Literacy in the Very Young." *School Library Journal* (July 1993): 28–31.

Kupetz, Barbara N., and Elise Jepson Green. "Sharing Books with Infants and Toddlers: Facing the Challenges." *Young Children* (January 1997): 22–27.

Nespeca, Sue McCleaf. "Bringing Up Baby." *School Library Journal* (November 1999): 49–52.

Soundy, Cathleen S. "Nurturing Literacy with Infants and Toddlers in Group Settings." *Childhood Education* (spring 1997): 149–55.

Teale, William H. "Libraries Promote Early Literacy Learning: Ideas from Current Research and Early Childhood Programs." *JOYS* (spring 1999): 9–18.

5 ENHANCEMENTS

You have selected books, rhymes, and poems that will be a wonderful introduction to the world of language for the very young child. Once your basic program outline is set up, you may want to enhance or add to it with a variety of language experiences for the children in addition to what they absorb with their sense of hearing. This is important because children use all their senses and are very tactile in their multiple ways of learning. The sections on using music, puppets, and flannel-board stories show how you can reinforce the language experience for the participants—visually, by using the sense of touch, and by physically involving the participants by dramatic play or acting out a rhyme. Entire books have been written about using music, puppets, and flannel-board stories in a story time, if you desire to immerse yourself in a specific field; this text will start you on your way.

The activities section contains ideas that can be taken home by the participants to do independently or that can be used as a group activity to end the program. These activities help make language-skills learning fun and again give ideas on how easy it is for the adult to help the child learn communication skills in everyday life. Creating displays will allow you to introduce services and materials that participants may not have time to research on their own and to make them aware of services they may not even know exist. Handouts can help them to recreate the world of language outside the program's boundaries and encourage them to continue language-skills learning experiences with the children on their own. Displays and handouts are also good ways to incorporate parent education into the program. You will find sample handouts included that may be used "as is" or adapted for use.

MUSIC

Children love to make and to listen to music. Of course, adults will often hear only the spoon banging on the tray, a bird chirping in a tree, or a little one babbling happily. Music has surrounded the child since the womb, with the heart beat and other sounds of the mother's body. Songs, chants, and rhymes are a way we can enhance the child's world through the sense of hearing. Even the hearing-impaired child can feel the rhythm by the vibrations of the beat. Studies have found that young children who are deaf will babble like any other children except they will use their hands instead of their voice (Golinkoff, 1999: 39–40).

Music can be used in many different ways throughout a program.

The presenter can "frame" the program by beginning and ending with the same song. Children will become familiar with this routine and often will settle down, focusing on the presenter and ready for the program when the song begins. Music can also be used as a transition tool as one moves from story book to another element in the program such as a bouncing rhyme. Transitional music or songs can also aid in collecting items you might have handed out. For example, when you have completed a song involving rhythm instruments such as shakers, you can use the following to aid the children in relinquishing them and putting them in a basket or other container. Sing to the tune of "Good Night Ladies" the following:

Good bye shakers.
Good bye shakers.
Good bye shakers.
We'll play another day.

It is amazing how this helps the children release the item. Some songs can be utilized as stories in themselves, and many have even been made into books. These popular song/stories are only a few examples of those that have been made into picture books: *If You're Happy and You Know It,* by David Carter; *Five Little Ducks,* by Raffi; *Old MacDonald Had a Farm,* by Frances Cony; and *Mary Had a Little Lamb,* photo-illustrated by Bruce McMillan.

Chanting is a form of music that many adults feel comfortable with, as some are self-conscious or severely critical of their singing ability. Needless to say, we are not all born with perfect pitch, and that is the very reason singing or chanting with children is so rewarding. The child is nonjudgmental and is amazed at the adult's skill and talent. Conveying this concept to parents can often lead to a breakthrough for them. Encouraging the adult to actively sing, chant, or just move to the music in the privacy of one's own home is one way the presenter can stress the importance of music in the child's life.

For the presenter, music can also be used to refocus the group back to the program at hand. A familiar song, such as "Wheels on the Bus," can encourage all present to take part in the actions. The familiar tune and beat of the music can direct attention back to the presenter. Soft music can also calm some situations such as a fussy or distracted child, especially when the accompanying adult sings along.

RHYTHM INSTRUMENTS

Rhythm instruments for this age group should be kept simple in design. Most important, please be very aware of safety issues. Do not let broken instruments or those with loose small pieces even be brought into the room. The best instruments for the 12-to-24-month-old to use independently are shakers, drums, and bells. These can be purchased from stores that support early childhood curricula or that are made by the presenter. If you intend to make them, remember to keep safety foremost in your mind.

Shakers

Shakers are often the simplest to make and can be put together in a variety of ways. Colored plastic eggs make bright and easy-to-hold shakers. Open the egg and place noise-making material inside of one half of the egg. This can be rice, dried beans, small rocks, or any other "shakable" material; different materials make different sounds, so experiment. Remember that the amount you put in will affect the sound. Run a small line of glue on the inside rim of the egg (a hot glue gun seems to work best). Put the two halves together, hold, and let set. You can cover the seam with colored electrical tape to reinforce the seal; this tape can be found in most hardware stores.

Another method of making shakers is to use prescription bottles with childproof lids. Select bottles that can be held comfortably without muffling the sound, and use ones that have no labels or else scrape most of the paper and tape off. Fill as you would the eggs and replace top securely. To decorate, you can use the colored electrical tape to cover the label area and signal dots or stickers to decorate the lid. Avery makes signal dots that are available at most office supply stores and come in numerous colors. Fun stickers can be found in card, craft, or curriculum stores and some department stores.

Pie-plate or tin-pan shakers will work, but be careful that all the edges are sealed so that the noise-making material cannot leak and there are no sharp edges or staples that might cause injury. These shakers may be a little more difficult for this age group to hold and shake properly.

Store these shakers in a box that has been decorated, a basket, or a mesh bag. The mesh bags are often laundry bags, which can be found in various colors and can be decorated. I have found the bag the fastest way to collect the shakers and store them.

Drums

Children love to drum—ask any adult who has listened to a child pounding on the highchair with a spoon for any length of time! Cooking pots, boxes, upside-down bowls, and even opened bags can become drums for a child with a wooden spoon or whatever else can be used as a drumstick, even the child's hand. It might be fair to warn you that some fledgling percussionist might consider shoes, tables, chairs, and even parts of the body suitable for drumming. To make simple drums for a group, the ever-ready coffee can is often the best bet. Remove any outer wrapper and wash out the can, drying it thoroughly. Decorate the outside with contact paper, stickers, or paint if you wish (if using paint be sure to use paint that contains no lead). Prior to replacing the top, you can put a line of glue around the outside rim of the can to ensure it staying in place. Each child can use a hand, a wooden spoon, or paint stirrer as a drumstick. Remember to check that drumming tools have no splinters or rough edges. If you are going to hand out drumsticks, the adults need to be reminded that this activity is one they need to do in conjunction with the child and be aware of safety.

Bells

The jingling of bells can brighten up anyone's day, and the delight little ones get out of making them ring is apparent all over their bodies. When using bells, make sure they are all safely fastened with no rough edges. School-supply stores and even toy stores handle these items. The usual shapes are either a ring with the bells fastened on the outside, or bells strung on a short stick; for this age group, I recommend the ring, for it is easy to grasp and manipulate. Elastic bands with bells securely sewn on, perhaps with fishing line, can be shaken by hand or slipped around the wrist or ankle of the child to make music while moving. For example, jumping up and down or marching in a circle would give a musical note to the activity, exercising large motor skills.

MEDIA

Using media to enhance the musical experience can be done in a variety of ways. Practice with the medium is essential, however, to ensure smooth transitions throughout the program. There are various media as well as a number of benefits from using each of them.

The most obvious medium is the boom-box. There is a difference between live and "canned" music, but both can be wonderful additions to a program. With the growing popularity of CDs, it is easier for the presenter to locate the correct music track. The machines themselves are becoming more compact, streamlined, and much more affordable. When using sound equipment, during the program be aware of the following tips:

1. Make sure the equipment is set up in a safe area where the children cannot upset it or be exposed to wiring.
2. Know the track number of the song if using a CD, or have the tape set to go so when you need to start the machine there is as little break in the program routine as possible. Use an index card to write the track number down to be certain you do not forget it.

3. Check the volume *before* turning on the machine. Unbeknownst to you, little fingers may have played with the volume control.

4. Actively involve the group in the music rather than just listen to it. The child may be held by the adult and rocked to the music; or the group can move as a whole by marching, swaying, or simply clapping along with the beat or even singing along. By starting and stopping the music, you can also create a game of start and stop, dance and freeze with very young children.

5. Unless you plan to devote the entire program to music, keep this section brief, or disperse the music portions throughout the whole program.

6. Using tapes and CDs does add a more dynamic music presentation, but beware of sound tracks where the language disappears under the musical score. One advantage of using your own voice is that it tends to be clearer and you can use just a simple melody that the participants can follow. An advantage to using tapes and CDs is that you have a backup for yourself if you need the support. An example of a useful tape is *Little Songs for Little Me* by Nancy Stewart. This music tape/CD has a solo voice singing the melody line, so one can clearly hear and understand the words accompanied by a simple guitar background.

VISUALS

Visual aids can illustrate a song, and many popular children's songs have been made into beautiful picture books. *Over in the Meadow* by John Langstaff has been available for years and is still loved by children. Raffi has put many of his songs into the picture-book format. Pop-up books are also fun to use when singing. *Old MacDonald Had a Farm,* by Frances Cony, and *If You're Happy and You Know It Clap Your Hands,* by David Carter, are just two books that work well in this type of presentation.

Picture cards can be as simple as a set of individual farm animals and one of a farmer. Picture cards can be created by using 8" x 11" sheets of paper on which you create pictures that reflect the song. This can be done by using a copy machine, by tracing, or by gluing actual pictures on paper. Use stiff paper or tag board in order to hold the picture card for easy viewing. Insert these into plastic page protectors or laminate them to increase their durability and make them sturdier for manipulation. Other visual aids include puppets and stuffed animals (see next section on puppets). When working with non-English speaking groups, visual aids enable the participants not only to learn the music but also to identify and name what is being sung about. An example of this is the "Animal Song" by Nancy Stewart found on her recording *Plant a Little Seed*. The words are as follows:

When ducks get up in the morning they always say good day.
When ducks get up in the morning they always say good day.
Quack, quack, quack, quack.
That is what they say.
They say quack, quack, quack, quack.
That is what they say!

In this song, then, by seeing the picture of a duck and hearing the word "duck" and the sound that ducks make, participants can make the connection between the animal identified and its English name. (Other animals may be substituted in place of "duck.")

Music is also useful in setting the tone of the program. Played prior to and after the program, it creates a relaxed atmosphere to encourage interaction between the adult and child as well as among the adults themselves. Background music of children's songs, folk melodies, classical, and other styles of music work well.

MATERIALS

Many of us enjoy incorporating music into our programs but have difficulty locating materials we can use. Not all of us have the ability to write original songs or even to create new lyrics to familiar children's songs that we already know. Two useful resource books are *The Children's Jukebox* (Reid, 1995) and *Growing Up with Music* (Sale, 1992). Although somewhat dated, especially the latter title, they can help you locate recordings for all ages, classical music, holiday recordings, and ESL materials. Both contain an index of song titles and discography.

Presenters may find it useful to observe a program where music is incorporated before they do it themselves. Videos can also be used to obtain new ideas on how to present traditional material. These videos, suitable for viewing in the home by adults to enjoy with their children, show music being used in group settings but also explain how to incorporate music at home. *Babies Make Music* is useful in that it shows the songs and music being incorporated into an actual group of adults with children infants to age three. It gives educational information concerning the purpose and use of the songs/rhymes/music in regards to child development. It is easy to include this information in your own program, making it not only fun but educational as well. Other good video sources are *Sally's From Wibbleton to Wobbleton* (Jaeger, 1998) and *Baby Songs* by Hap Palmer and the Wee Sing videos.

Everyone eventually discovers a favorite recording, artist, or song that always works in their program. The following materials offer a few ideas to get you started in learning about recording artists, recordings you might enjoy using, and Websites you might want to investigate.

Recordings

Let's Sing Fingerplays, by Tom Glazer.
Baby Games, by Priscilla Hegner.
Burl Ives Sings Little White Duck and Other Children's Favorites, by Burl Ives.
Baby Record, by Bob McGrath and Sarah Smithrim.
Baby Songs, by Hap Palmer.
Hap Palmer Sings Classic Nursery Rhymes, by Hap Palmer.
Little Songs for Little Me, by Nancy Stewart.
Plant a Little Seed, by Nancy Stewart.
   Performers to keep an ear out for:

Peter, Paul and Mary	Hap Palmer
Sharon, Lois and Bram	Woodie Guthrie
Ella Jenkins	Pete Seeger
Nancy Raven	Pat Carfra
Tom Glazer	Raffi
Bob McGrath	Nancy Stewart
Wee Sing	

RESOURCES FOR MUSIC

There are numerous resources that will encourage and aid you in incorporating music into your program. One of the newest is Jackie Silberg's book *I Can't Sing Book for Grownups Who Can't Carry a Tune in a Paper Bag . . . But Want to Do Music with Young Children* (1998). Quite a mouthful, but it's very useful with simple guidelines to introduce children to music via rhythm, sound language, movement, instruments, and actual activities to do with songs. Geared more toward the two year old and up, Silberg does supply appropriate age-group levels for each activity. The book is also a good source for activities that can be done by the adult and child outside the program's boundaries.

   For a more in-depth study, *Music: A Way of Life for the Young Child,* by Kathleen Bayless and Marjorie Ramsey (1991), is a good choice. Part 1 focuses on music in the earliest years, covering infancy to three years old. It describes characteristics of the child, musical skills that can be evident at each age level, and how to introduce and enhance the musical experience for the child. Suggested readings, song collections, recordings, and resources make this very useful. Part 2 covers the preschooler and kindergartner. Part 3 explores music in the daily life of children, from learning situations to just plain fun. Information concerning the child with special needs is in this section, including creating a less restrictive environment, general suggestions, and techniques for handling the unique child with special needs, as well as references and suggested readings. Appendices include musical notation, instructions for playing the autoharp, and a subject and song index.

There are other books that include sections on music as an activity that includes both the child and adult. These can be used in programming as idea books. *Games to Play with Toddlers* (Silberg, 1993) is uniquely organized to aid in locating the kind of games available, the appropriate age to play the game, as well as what the game is reinforcing. Since music can be incorporated as a learning experience, rhythm experience, language-skill builder, and fun experience, there are many opportunities to involve music in daily life; Silberg devotes an entire chapter to art and singing games. Each section lists the games and what the toddler will learn, along with the given designated-age groups: 12 to 15 months, 15 to 18 months, 18 to 21 months, and 21 to 24 months. Both *Things to Do with Toddlers and Twos* (Miller, 1984) and *More Things to Do with Toddlers and Twos* (Miller, 1994) incorporate music and rhythm instruments in the activities provided. You can also refer to the Resources section for Rhymes, Fingerplays, and Songs, in chapter 4.

Books and Videos

Briggs, Diane. *101 Fingerplays, Stories, and Songs to Use with Finger Puppets*. Chicago: American Library Association, 1999.

Chadha, Nisha. *Multicultural Book of Songs*. London: Mantra, 1994.

Chorao, Kay. *Knock at the Door and Other Baby Action Rhymes*. New York: Dutton, 1999.

Davis, Sandra Carpenter. *Bounce Me Tickle Me Hug Me: Lap Rhymes and Play Rhymes from Around the World*. Toronto: Parent-Child Mother Goose Program, 1997. (The rhymes are printed in their original languages, with English translations and directions.)

Defty, Jeff. *Creative Fingerplays and Action Rhymes. An Index and Guide to Their Use*. Phoenix, Ariz.: Oryx, 1992.

Dunn, Opal. *Hippety-Hop, Hippety Hay! Growing with Rhymes from Birth to Age Three*. New York: Henry Holt, 1999.

Glazer, Tom. *Music for Ones and Twos: Songs and Games for the Very Young Child*. New York: Doubleday, 1983.

Griego, Margot, et al., comps. and trans. *Tortillitas Para Mama and Other Nursery Rhymes. Spanish and English*. New York: Holt, Rinehart and Winston, 1981.

Jaeger, Sally. *Sally's From Wibbleton to Wobbleton*. Video, 40 minutes. 49 North Productions, Toronto, 1998.

Kleiner, Lynn, and Dennis Devine, prods. and dirs. *Babies Make Music*. Video, 52 minutes. Music Rhapsody, Redondo Beach, Calif, 1996.

McGrath, Bob. *The Baby Record*. Bob McGrath and Katharine Smithrim. Racine, Wis.: Golden, 1990. Cassette: Golden Music 41007-01; CD: Bob's Kids Music 41007-03.

————. *Songs and Games for Toddlers.* Bob McGrath and Katharine Smithrim. Cambridge, Ont.: Golden, 1990. Cassette: Bob's Kids Music 41016-01; CD: Bob's Kids Music 41016-03.

Orozco, Jose-Luis. *Diez Deditos: Ten Little Fingers and Other Play Rhymes and Action Songs from Latin America.* New York: Dutton, 1997.

Palmer, Hap. *Baby Songs.* Video, 30 minutes. Los Angeles: Hi-Tops Video, 1987.

Reid, Rob. *Children's Jukebox: A Subject Guide to Musical Recordings and Programming Ideas for Songsters Ages One to Twelve.* Chicago: American Library Association, 1995.

Sale, Laurie. *Growing Up with Music: A Guide to the Best Recorded Music for Children.* New York: Avon, 1992. (This book is dated but still useful.)

Scott, Anne. *The Laughing Baby: Remembering Nursery Rhymes and Reasons.* New York: Bergin and Garvey, 1987.

Silberg, Jackie. *Games to Play with Toddlers.* Beltsville, Md.: Gryphon House, 1993.

————. *I Can't Sing Book for Grownups Who Can't Carry a Tune in a Paper Bag . . . But Want to Do Music with Young Children.* Beltsville, Md.: Gryphon House, 1998.

Stewart, Nancy. *Little Songs for Little Me: Activity Songs for Ones and Twos.* Sound recording. Friends Street Music, 1992.

————. *Plant a Little Seed: Songs for Growing Children.* Sound recording. Friends Street Music, 1995.

Websites

These are Internet sites with ideas and information on recordings in the field of children's music.

www.bestchildrensmusic.com	Gives reviews of recordings.
www.funmusicideas.com	Fun Music Ideas site. Advice and links to other sites, free monthly newsletter.
www.childrensmusic.org	Children's Music Web. A nonprofit organization dedicated to music for kids, ties to other related organizations such as Children's Music Network. Covers research on music and the brain.
www.cmnonline.org	Children's Music Network. A nonprofit organization with members in the U.S. and Canada that share songs and ideas about children's music, how to communicate

through music, and the use of music for education and community building.

www.childrensmusichouse.com — Children's Music House began as a distributor in 1980 serving public libraries and schools. Supplies recorded music, videos, audiobooks, read alongs, and DVDs.

www.kimboed.com — Kimbo Education is a specialty recording company which publishes music for all ages on cassette, CD, video, and LP primarily aimed at young children.

www.2-life.com/meyc — Music Education for Young Children WebSite. This is a Website provided by Deborah Pratt as a resource for teachers and parents covering books, games, catalogs, teaching ideas, topics such as "Music and the Brain" and others related to music and children.

www.nancymusic.com — Nancy Stewart homepage. Website of award-winning professional musician and songwriter. Site includes activity pages for making homemade instruments, games to play with music, how to share music with babies, and links to sites related to music and children. Contact: Friends Street Music, 6505 28th, Mercer Island, WA 98040 or call (206) 232-1078.

www.musicrhapsody.com — Music Rhapsody. Based on Orff-Schulwerk philosophy of music, Music Rhapsody was created by Lynn Kleiner for children from infants to grade 8. Music is taught through active participation, instruments, imagination, and props such as scarves. Suggested ideas for getting started introducing music to children are covered.

members.tripod.com/~ESL4Kids — The EFL Playhouse site. A resource for teachers of young learners. Information about working with ESL families and materials to use.

FLANNEL BOARDS

Flannel boards, felt boards, and magnetic boards are all useful when doing a program with the 12-to-24-month age group. With large groups, this kind of story presentation enables better visibility and attracts the audience's attention. It is best to keep the number of pieces to a minimum, to outline rather than give lots of detail, and to use bold colors. There are many sizes of boards, and one must try them out to find which one best suits your style of storytelling. The board itself can vary in size from 9" x 12" to the size of an artist's portfolio. I have found the smaller size easier to keep out of little hands; it is also less distracting when not in use. The larger ones of course allow for more and larger pieces, but remember you will want to put it aside when the story is finished. Judy Sierra (1997) includes directions for making different kinds of flannel boards as well as a mitt flannel board, which has the advantage of being able to be moved so all may see the presentation. The thing to remember is that the smaller the board, the smaller the pieces.

There are alternatives to using a flannel board for presentation. You can use a mitt format, with a glove made of the proper material or even a garden glove or rubber glove with Velcro on the tips. You can also purchase or make aprons that have a nap conducive to "sticking." Information on how to make small individual flannel boards for your group can be found on the handout entitled "Flannel Board Fun" at the end of this chapter.

It takes time and effort to create flannel-board pieces. This is true if you enlarge or copy the patterns on paper and color them or use material and glue. Many people make copies of the pieces they desire, color them in, and laminate them for durability. Laminating machines are becoming more accessible and compact. Check with the schools in your area or curriculum stores to see if they will let you laminate gratis or for a fee. Alternatively, paper pieces can be placed between two pieces of clear contact paper, with the sticky sides together, and then pressed flat.

Once the pieces are made, you need to be able to store them for easy access and protection. Trying to find missing pieces is not the best way to prepare for a program. File folders with closed sides work well and come in a variety of sizes. Each rhyme/story set can have its own labeled file to keep the pieces together that is stored in a file cabinet. "Zippered" plastic bags can also be used for storage, but since they are slippery they may not stand up, so box storage may work better—or materials can be placed in hanging files in the file cabinet. You can also store the pieces in a loose-leaf binder if you place the pieces in plastic page protectors. Be aware that this storage method does have size limitations when making your pieces. The binder can also include an index of the rhymes/songs stored there, thus helping you find them easily.

Many rhymes and songs are easy to adapt for flannel boards, allowing for variations in presenting the rhyme or song. Sierra (1997) has fourteen different rhymes, chants, and songs for the youngest children included in her *The Flannel Board Storytelling Book*. The pattern pieces are simple and easy to make. *Flannelboard Stories for Infants and Toddlers* by Ann Carlson and Mary Carlson (1999) offers additional story ideas that can be presented using the flannel board. Other pattern resources are listed following this section.

Following are stories and rhymes from the annotated bibliography and list found in chapter 4 that can be presented in flannel-board format:

> *Ask Mr. Bear*, by Marjorie Flack
> *Big Fat Worm*, by Nancy Van Laan
> *Blue Sea*, by Robert Kalan
> *The Box with Red Wheels*, by Maud and Miska Petersham
> *Brown Bear, Brown Bear*, by Bill Martin
> *The Carrot Seed*, by Ruth Krauss
> *Five Little Pumpkins*, by Iris Van Rynbach
> *Freight Train*, by Donald Crews
> *Here Is the Engine* (traditional rhyme)
> *How Do I Put It On?* by Shigeo Wantanabe
> *I Went Walking*, by Sue Williams
> *Let's Go Visiting*, by Sue Williams
> *My Many Colored Days*, by Dr. Seuss
> *Now We Can Go*, by Ann Jonas
> *Oh, A-Hunting We Will Go*, by John Langstaff
> *Old MacDonald Had a Farm* (traditional rhyme)
> *Over in the Meadow*, by John Langstaff
> *Whose Hat?* by Margaret Miller

RESOURCES FOR FLANNEL BOARDS
Books

Carlson, Ann, and Mary Carlson. *Flannelboard Stories for Infants and Toddlers*. Chicago: American Library Association, 1999.

Sierra, Judy. *The Flannel Board Storytelling Book*. 2d ed. New York: Wilson, 1997.

Pattern Sources

Totline Magazine
P.O. Box 2250
Everett, WA 98203
800-264-9873   e-mail: totline@get.net

CopyCat Magazine
P.O. Box 081546
Racine, WI 53408-1546
www.copycatpress.com

PUPPETS

Many a child's face lights up with delight at the sight of a puppet. There is an immediate connection between the child and this creation. Most of the time the usual reaction is a positive one, but on occasion the child can be frightened or upset by the appearance of a puppet. When using puppets with this age group, keep in mind a number of things.

First of all, the child will likely grab for the puppet or try to reach it. Usually this is because they want to make sure the adult they are with sees it too. I have seen puppets being walked all over the room by children who want to share the puppet with the other participants or want to keep it for themselves. If you use a large puppet, especially as a host puppet, you might want to keep it up out of reach when not using it as a demonstration model for yourself. By putting it down on a chair or low table, you are inviting the children to come and meet it. This can cause the group to become distracted.

Second, keep in mind the size of puppet you feel comfortable with. If you use an oversized puppet as a demonstration tool, you must be competent in manipulating it. Smaller puppets, such as finger puppets, can "disappear" when you are finished with them into a container or your pocket. Size does not always ensure everything works smoothly, however. I've had a little blackbird fingerpuppet "fly" out into the group, and it had to be caught before the program could continue. Whatever size you use, make sure you practice with the puppet prior to the program.

The third concept is to be wary of incorporating too many puppets into your program. It is tempting to liven up your programs with various puppets among the different materials you may use, but using many different puppets for the various parts of your program means you have to have them available. You have to have a place to hold them when not in use, and they may give the children too many things to focus on at one time. Be aware of overstimulating the children or giving them "too much of a good thing." Perhaps you can use the same puppet various times throughout the program. Or would it work better if you always have one puppet for the program and introduce others throughout the series? Children like the familiar and will grow accustomed and comfortable with a puppet that is used repeatedly.

The fourth thing to remember is to watch the children's reactions to the puppet and take your cue from them. Let the children approach the puppet, if that is your intention. Children are often wary of puppets until they recognize them as "friends," so take the introduction slowly, and it can lead to a wonderful relationship between child and puppet-friend.

Finally, make sure your puppet will stay together. It's very upsetting to a child to hug a host puppet and have its head come off. Puppets that are made professionally are often sturdy enough, as are many handmade ones. There are many books that contain patterns or ideas on how to make puppets on the market; see the recommended books at the end of this section for specific titles. When you make puppets to use for these programs, remember that children this age will often put things in their mouths. Be aware of small pieces and objects you may use, and make sure they are firmly attached.

What can puppets be used for in programming for this age group? Often they are used as host puppets or as a demonstration model. In this manner, the puppet is the presenter's "child" to demonstrate fingerplays and action rhymes. Puppets can also be used to act out rhymes, fingerplays, songs, or even stories. If actual puppets are unavailable, stuffed toys can also be used in this way. For example, the ever-popular Bill Martin story *Brown Bear, Brown Bear* has a variety of ways in which it can be brought to life with action. You can make a stick-puppet theater or use stuffed toys to represent each animal character as the story is recited or read. In this manner, the participants will hear a familiar story being presented in a variety of ways. The presenter, on the other hand, will be able to keep the story fresh by varying the presentation while staying true to the story.

RESOURCES FOR PUPPETS
Books

Briggs, Diane. *101 Fingerplays, Stories and Songs to Use with Finger Puppets.* Chicago: American Library Association, 1999.

Hunt, Tamara, and Nancy Renfro. *Pocketful of Puppets: Mother Goose.* Austin, Tex.: Nancy Renfro Studios, 1982a.

————. *Puppetry in Early Childhood Education.* Austin, Tex.: Nancy Renfro Studios, 1982b.

Rottman, Fran. *Easy-to-Make Puppets and How to Use Them.* Ventura, Calif.: Gospel Light, 1995.

Where to Find Puppets

Toy stores
Local craft bazaars

Folkmanis Puppets
   1219 Park Ave.
   Emeryville, CA 94608 USA
   www.folkmanis.com
Nancy Renfro Studios
   www.fc.net/~puppets
   toll free: 800-933-5512
Library supply catalogs such as:
   Upstart
   toll free: 800-448-4887
   www.highsmith.com
(Upstart is a division of Highsmith, Inc.—from homepage click on "Highsmith, Inc.," then "Library Supplies & Equipment," then "shop.")
Demco
   toll free: 800-962-4463
   www.demco.com
Early education supply catalogs and stores such as:
   Lakeshore Learning Materials
   toll free: 800-428-4414
   www.lakeshorelearning.com
ABC School Supply
   toll free: 800-669-4422
   www.abcschoolsupply.com

ACTIVITIES

WHY PLAN ACTIVITIES?

Children learn about their world by using all their senses. Activities can be used within the program itself or as suggested things to follow up on at home. Such activities can help to build language skills since the adult can talk to the child about what is being done, felt, smelled, seen, and heard. Within the program, these activities should be at the conclusion so that the child/adult pair may spend as much time as they desire on the project. The at-home portion of the language-building experience can continue outside the library. Remember, it is the learning *process* of the activity that is important, not the end result. Open-ended activities that allow for creativity, dialog, and exploration are best. Encourage the adult to actively participate with the child in the activity but to be careful not to direct the child as to what to do. It takes children this age time to examine and process what they are doing in order to learn. The adult should allow the child time to respond either with an action or by using language, be it body language or verbal. At this stage of development, children learn through all their senses; they are very tactile, and learning this way also reinforces what they hear and see. They are learning to associate meanings with the sounds they hear around them and are becoming aware these sounds/words are used to identify, direct, and communicate.

Choose activities that the adults can participate in and thereby model the skill necessary so they can help the children learn. Making these activities fun will also encourage the participants to recreate the experience again and again. All the activities listed can be language-building ones as long as the adult and child "talk" to each other, thereby beginning to build the communication bridge. When supplying activities, remember to be aware of safety issues involved—for example, if the children are still putting everything in their mouths, you will need to select the appropriate activity with nontoxic materials, and that all these activities need a caring, proactive adult involved with the child to ensure an enriching experience.

The following activities are divided into two basic groups: activities to perform and activities that are arts-and-crafts related.

ACTION ACTIVITIES
Water Related
Children love to play with water.

- Give them different temperatures or forms of water (warm, cold, ice) and use words to describe them. For example, "The ice is slippery and cold."
- Give them simple "toys" to use in the bathtub such as a nonbreakable measuring cup or funnel.
- Give a baby doll a bath, or perhaps help wash vegetables for eating.
- Fill a dishpan or sink with water and give the child different objects to see which ones float or sink.
- Use bubbles to hide an object in the water, or float boats on the surface.
- Use a sponge to soak up water, and let the child discover what happens when it's squeezed.

Outings

- Visit a zoo, farm, grocery store, garden, nursery with lots of different flowers, a playground—the locales are endless. You might even read a story about such places before and after you go.
- Go for a walk—around the house, around the block, in the rain,

to a park—anywhere. Talk about what you see, hear, feel, smell, and so on.

- When driving, be a tour guide for your child. Describe where you are going, what you see along the way, what you may do once you get there. You can even make going to the laundromat an adventure.
- Get down close to the grass and look at it. Talk about what creatures you may find.
- Plant a garden. It does not have to be big at all, perhaps just in a small container. The child can even plant seeds in a cup, but be sure the seeds go in the cup, not the mouth.
- Take a walk on bubble wrap. Talk about the sounds, the surface, its characteristics.
- Collect leaves, rocks, whatever, on your walk. Talk about what they look like, feel like, perhaps even sound like.

Imagination Play

Children this age should not be expected to know how to "play," so it is best if the adult can be a role model, playing alongside the child to facilitate learning.

- Have a telephone conversation using a toy phone.
- Trains and trucks are fun to drive and manipulate. Create a ramp by using a cookie sheet, cardboard, or large wrapping/mailing cardboard tube to roll objects through. Such objects may be plastic "wiffle" golf balls, trucks, or even a stuffed toy. Adult can talk about size, speed, where is it, and the like.
- Get a large-sized box and help the child create a boat, house, cave, wagon, or other environment with it.
- Large mirrors are fascinating to the very young child. Allow the child to use a large safety mirror (unbreakable) to discover body parts as well as see facial reactions.
- Blow feathers, leaves, scarves, or bubbles. Talk about textures, types of wind (hard, soft, strong).
- Create a flannel board by covering cardboard (8" x 11" or any size) with felt or flannel; you can also use the inside cover of a clean pizza box. Cut out simple shapes free hand or use cookie cutters for outlines, and have the child create stories and learn hand-to-eye coordination as well. Pictures from coloring books, magazines, and even photos may be mounted on felt or flannel. Store pieces in a "zippered" bag, a box, or inside the pizza box.
- The wooden spoon has been the basis for many a puppet for the young child by simply decorating it as a face. Mittens can be handled the same way. Craft sticks, tongue depressors, straws

or stirrer sticks can create stick puppets. Simply place a sticker at one end or use a marker to draw a face on it. You can also mount pictures from magazines or photos on sturdy paper and then glue them on one end of the stick. Larger puppets, often commercially made, are great to use with the very young child. They encourage interaction between the child and puppet, who often "talk" together without shyness.

- Play peek-a-boo. Draping chiffon scarves or other see-through material over the head, the adult can disappear and then reappear. When placed over the child's head, the see-through material is reassuring. Cover an object such as a stuffed toy, doll, or truck with the scarf and then make it reappear. Remember to talk about the object and what is happening.
- Hide and Go Seek is best when the very young child is the one who hides. Make sure the adult talks while looking for the child. "Now where is Billy? I am going to look behind the chair." Many times the child will pop out from their hiding place, bringing the game to a halt. The adult should react with appropriate surprise and joy.

Language

These activities are all related to language building and literacy.

- Greeting cards are wonderful things. Use ones that have no small, loose pieces or glitter on them. Take a collection of cards and place them in a dishpan or box. The child will enjoy taking them out, putting them in, opening and closing them, as well as looking at them. You can create stories about the pictures or just describe what is on them. Identify objects, animals, flowers, and anything else depicted.
- Junk mail is fun for the child and adult to talk about and sort. Help create the letter-writing habit in the child by helping to "write" a letter to someone and then mail it. Involve the child in the whole process and talk about what you are doing: getting paper, writing, addressing, post office, mailbox, and so on.
- Plastic can covers are great to help develop eye-to-hand control and coordination. Using fine motor skills, the child can pick up a can cover and place in a box or coffee can. If you make a slit or hole in the top of the container, the child can "mail" the juice cover. Children love the sound the lid makes when it is dropped in. Colorful stickers are fun to put on these juice lids, or you can use signal dots available at most office supply stores. Later on the lids can be used in a sorting game or identification game.
- Create picture cards using index cards. Simply glue pictures or use stickers to cover the card, then lay it picture side down on

clear contact paper (cover both sides of the card if so desired). Cut apart cards and these picture cards may be used in the same manner as the greeting cards or juice lids.

- Make your own books. Photo albums, especially the magnetic kind, allow for pictures to be moved and words written on the pages. Make a book about the child taking photos of the daily routine. By placing thin cardboard in a plastic food-storage bag, you can create a two-sided page that can then be sewn together with others using strong thread or yarn, making a book—though not as sturdy as the first type.

- Play dress up. This does not mean you have to go out and buy these clothes. Children can be creative with scarves, hats, old slips, shoes, and the like. Don't put out a trunk load of clothes either. The very young child does not need an unlimited number of things to select from, but just a few.

- Create a playspace. Small pop-up tents have become popular to use, but a sheet works just as well. Just make sure that it is draped securely over objects that will not fall over and cause injuries.

- Give the child her own catalog to help her practice turning pages. Repetition is an essential part of learning. It is much better to practice on an old catalog, probably ripping pages, than a beautiful picture book.

- With your child, look at magazines, books, and other objects where words and pictures are found together. Talk about what you see and let your child take time to absorb as much on the page as desired. Reading time may be limited to only one page, but that is how it all begins.

- Let your child handle and discover different kinds of paper by crunching it into a ball, tearing it, examining it. Use regular paper, wax paper, cardboard, newspaper—any kind.

- Music can play a large part in the language learning of children. There are many rhymes and songs that reflect the daily activities of a very young child. Create rhythm instruments from pots, wooden spoons, plastic bowls, empty coffee cans, and things around the house.

- Exercise time is a wonderful time to use language, especially songs that make the activity fun for both the adult and child. Roll a ball back and forth between the child and adult. Use two different-sized balls (make the size difference distinct) or different colors and talk about concepts such as bounce high, low, color, fast, slow.

- When baking, read the recipe to the child and name the ingredients and utensils as you get them out. Allow the child to decorate cookies, cupcakes (mini ones are best), or graham crackers with icing, fruit jam, or even peanut butter on a small plastic knife or ice cream stick.

- Puzzles are fun at this age as long as pieces are large and the number kept to a minimum. See the arts-and-crafts section for making puzzles.

ARTS AND CRAFTS

When doing arts-and-crafts projects with this age group, it is important to remember a few things.

1. It is the process that is important, not the end result.
2. The child is the creator, and the adult needs to allow the child to do the activity. Materials for the adults to use to create as well may be helpful to have. Children like to do what they see the adult doing.
3. Allow for room to move around. Large motor skills are used during this time period rather than fine motor skills. Big pieces of paper, chunky crayons, large pieces are all necessary for the child to feel successful in creating and to avoid frustration.
4. Messes will happen, it is inevitable. Remind the adult it is all about how the child is learning about the world. Hands need to "dig in." Old clothes, drop cloths, and a sense of play are important. If making a mess is not desired, then select the activities that involve action rather than arts-and-crafts materials. There are, however, some arts-and-crafts activities that can be adapted to minimize messes, such as the "squish bag," which is a portable and much less messy form of finger painting: The finger-painting material is encased inside a zippered freezer bag. See the section on "Paint" later in this chapter for directions on how to make them.
5. All materials should be nontoxic. Children are still putting things in their mouths. There are recipes for paint, playdough, glue, and others that are all safe.
6. There needs to be a caring, involved adult with the child during every activity. Encourage the adult to talk to the child about what is happening, to respond verbally to the child, and to provide the opportunity to respond. Keep the exchange positive in nature and not critical. Remind the adult that, just as in a reading experience, the child needs time to respond and to proceed at a unique pace. Resources for recipes and idea books are given at the end of this section. Check the sample handouts for some basic recipes as well.

Playdough

Homemade playdough is not very hard or time consuming to make. Kept in the refrigerator, it lasts quite a while. Playing with it at different temperatures gives lots of opportunity for language use with descriptions of soft, hard, cold, warm, and the like. The edible forms are less stressful if your child is still tasting things. Use food coloring to make different-colored dough, and even give the child two different colors to create a third color dough. Adding flavorings makes this an activity for the sense of smell to explore, as well—vanilla, cinnamon, and other scents are fun to use. Children can stick things into playdough such as fake flowers, toy animals, and straws, and use cookie cutters with the dough.

Paint

Children will more than likely use their hands rather than a paint brush to paint. Many times their surface for painting will include the highchair tray, the floor or walls, and themselves. Water is often a good "paint" to use inside or outside during warm weather—let them paint the house, sidewalk, and rocks, to name just a few places. For the youngest ones, put a small amount of applesauce, babyfood carrots, or other colored food on the highchair tray and let the child create.

If this is too messy for you, create a "squish bag" out of a plastic freezer bag by putting inside it a substitute finger paint. This can be instant pudding that has been made with half the amount of liquid (substitute water for milk), whipped cream, or any mushy food. Vanilla pudding and white whipped cream can change color by simply adding food coloring, and chocolate pudding makes great "dirt." Fill the bag with a small amount, 2 tablespoons to $1/4$ cup, depending on the bag size, being careful not to overfill. The bag should be able to lie flat without showing the entire surface under it. Press the air out gently and zip the bag tightly closed. Reinforce all four sides with tape; masking tape and duct tape work best. Children can move the "finger paint" around inside the bag and create patterns by pressing their fingers or hands on the bag's surface. This gives them a visual and tactile experience; it gives you a portable, nonmessy, finger-painting bag. Safety tip: remember to keep the bag out of child's mouth.

Paint can be put into pie pans for easy access; make sure the child can reach the painting surface easily. Low, child-level tables are good, or, if in a group, place closed-up folding tables on the floor for a contained surface. To apply the paint, there are many kinds of brushes available as well as other painting tools. Use sponges, daubers (available at arts-and-crafts supply stores), fingers, the wheels of toy trucks, feathers, rollers, and other items as painting tools.

Coloring

Use large paper whenever possible. It can be cut into shapes or used as is. Chalk works well on dark colors, and white paper is great for all colors.

Glue

First, some tips: Water and flour are the simplest ingredients for glue, though glue sticks may cut down on the mess if the child can manipulate them well enough. Q-tips may be used to apply the glue; gluing requires an adult with the child to insure safety and assist the child before frustration sits in, since glue situations can become too sticky! The adult may have to assist in applying the glue, and then the child can place the materials to be glued.

Collages are a wonderful medium that lets children create their own masterpieces. Colored paper, different types of paper, feathers, fabric, cotton balls—use your imagination—are all useful materials for creating collages. A simpler glue project is to use stickers instead of glue.

To create a color experience without crayons, paint, or the like, use colored cellophane paper or colored acetate report folders. They enable the child to see the world in a different light and supply lots of opportunity for dialog with the adult. Safety tip: Be sure cellophane stays out of the mouth, as it could endanger breathing.

Clear contact paper creates a sticky surface for the child to glue things to without too much mess. Tape the contact paper sticky side up on a surface such as the refrigerator door, the floor, a table top, the lower portion of the wall, or even a good size piece of cardboard. Then give the child things to glue such as paper, feathers, pompoms, and the like.

Create puzzles by gluing a picture drawn by you or the child to a piece of sturdy cardboard or even foam board. The thicker material makes it easier for the child to pick up. Cut the puzzle into no more than four pieces, and do not make the cuts too complicated. More complicated puzzles can be created as the child grows in ability to put the puzzles together.

Once given the start, you or another adult can often begin thinking up language skill-building activities to share with the child. Just as in reading, take cues from the child in order for these activities to be successful events for all involved.

RESOURCES FOR ACTIVITIES

Catlin, Cynthia. *More Toddlers Together: The Complete Planning Guide for a Toddler Curriculum.* Vol. 2. Beltsville, Md.: Gryphon House, 1996.

————. *Toddlers Together.* Beltsville, Md.: Gryphon House, 1994.

Hodges, Susan. *Toddler Art.* Torrance, Calif.: Totline, 1998.

Kohl, MaryAnn F. *Mudworks: Creative Clay, Dough and Modeling Experiences.* Bellingham, Wash.: Bright Ring, 1989.

Martin, Elaine. *Baby Games.* Philadelphia, Penna.: Running Press, 1988.

Miller, Karen. *More Things to Do with Toddlers and Twos*. Chelsea, Mass.: TelShare, 1994.

————. *Things to Do with Toddlers and Twos*. Chelsea, Mass.: TelShare, 1984.

Silberg, Jackie. *Games to Play with Babies*. Rev. and exp. ed. Beltsville, Md.: Gryphon House, 1993.

————. *Games to Play with Toddlers*. Beltsville, Md.: Gryphon House, 1993.

Staso, William H. *Brain under Construction: Experiences that Promote the Intellectual Capabilities of Young Toddlers*. Book 2 of a series: 8–18 Months. Orcutt, Calif.: Great Beginnings, 1997.

DISPLAYS

Displays enable you to spotlight materials, services, and ideas that you want to make the participants aware of, and can be as simple or as elaborate as you desire. They also help you add an education component to your program depending on what and where the display materials are. If the display is in the same area as the program, it is more likely to be looked at than if it is located elsewhere. It is important to remember that the adult will have a very young child along, which may limit the ability to browse. Make sure to post a "Check these out" sign on or near the display area, since many adults may need a reminder to check out library material and not just walk off with it. When planning displays, keep in mind the following:

1. Where will the display be and how large? Most displays are on tables, out of the reach of curious little hands. Small tables, such as card tables, can often be used instead of oversized ones. The top of a bookcase or shelf would work, though, if it is at the right height—at least 36" high. Is there room in the program area, preferably by the entrance/exit and away from the program proper? Place the display where it will cause the least amount of distraction during the program. For safety reasons, don't use a tablecloth, since children this age in practicing standing and walking, might grab onto the cloth and bring it and the display down on top of themselves. If space does not allow for even a small display, create one outside the program area and tell the participants about it, encouraging them not only to go out and look at it but also to explore the library/facility itself. An informal "tour" on the way might help them to become acquainted with the area as well. If this program is going to be

done outside the library itself, check with that location's facilitator about setting up a display.

2. Exactly how much time does the librarian/presenter have to gather together display materials? In reality, in a relatively short matter of time one can select books from the collection that parents/caregivers/children will find useful. Displays are meant to be a sampling, not everything on a subject. If a specific topic is desired for the display, one may want to collect material over a period of time. Exorbitant amounts of time are not necessary to create one, and often a quick walk through the library stacks is enough to gather sufficient material.

IDEAS FOR DISPLAYS

Displays can be used to educate the participants about many things. Here are ten ideas to get you started:

1. Parenting books: include categories such as general parenting, adoption, discipline, the working parent, and communicating with the child.
2. Books that support the adult: gather information on things to do with the child, places to go in the area, (park district information booklets, for example), self-help books, arts-and-crafts books, how to start a play group, how to pick a day care or preschool, and other valuable areas.
3. Child-development books, early brain-development books, resources for assistance and learning for the parent can also support the adult.
4. Magazines: those such as *Parenting* and *Family Fun* are aimed directly at the adult and family. *Ladybug*, a magazine for the very young child, or any early childhood education magazines in your collection are good also. Subscriptions to such magazines can be expensive and having access to them through the library is a definite plus for adults with limited funds.
5. Special collections that the participants need to be aware of: for example, advertise circulating puppets or toys, or provide special handouts such as lists of books that have been created specifically with this age child in mind.
6. Appropriate books for the very young child: select materials that demonstrate good qualities to use reading aloud. There is such a variety of board books now that this kind of display is not only easy to create but colorful as well. Actually seeing, examining, and using books that work well with this age group will help the adult recognize others.
7. Variations of materials. Mother Goose has always been popular reading material for this age group, but today there are many

variations available with all styles of illustrations. Display other poetry books in addition to Mother Goose. *Catch Me and Kiss Me and Say it Again* by Watson (1978), *Read-Aloud Poems for the Very Young* by Jack Prelutzky (1986) are only a couple of the wonderful poetry books now out. ABC books are popular, so *26 Letters & 99 Cents* by Tana Hoban (1987), Wanda Gag's *ABC Bunny* (1933), and Bill Martin's *Chicka Chicka, Boom Boom* (1989) can be used to focus on that.

8. Set up award-winning books, old favorites that the adults may recognize from their own childhood, or selected books that reflect the theme of the program.

9. Books that make "a good home library" for the child and family. For this I have even gathered up books from my daughter's collection to show the adults. It often reassures them it is all right for board books, cloth or vinyl books, and books of lesser literary quality to be included. It will also remind them that books that are worn and well loved have value, too.

10. Various types of nonprint material. Display quality recordings available in tape and CD formats. Videos that are fun viewing for adult and child are also good to display, reminding the adults they are to be viewed by the adult and child together. Does your library circulate art work or other materials that adults may use at home, such as books on tape? Do not forget to include materials that help the adult select these materials, such as magazines that review them and books that help them use and incorporate them into their daily lives. Having a tape/CD player available allows the adults to preview a selection.

Displays are not absolutely necessary, but they offer a great way to inform and educate the participants. It also makes for easier browsing by the adult, since the materials have been preselected. As with handouts, displays are visual indicators to the participants that they are valuable to the library and worth the extra effort made by the library/facility to make this language experience the best possible for them and their child.

HANDOUTS

At the same time it seems as if participants always want more handouts, there always seem to be too many to read. There are so many topics important to serving this age child that those who receive handouts as well as the people who have to prepare and create them can become overwhelmed. The time involved in creating handouts must be balanced with their value to those they are intended to serve. Handouts should be kept simple and easy to understand in order for them to be utilized effectively. Quite often, these handouts are introductions rather than an end in and of themselves. They can include fingerplays, guidelines for programs, child-development points, reasons to read to your child, suggested books for the very young child, and evaluations for programs.

Many libraries and organizations have a variety of handouts that can inform participants of services. The following are handouts that should be available at each program to encourage the non-library user to begin utilizing the public library and its resources:

1. the library's hours. This is important so the adult can know when access to your facility is available. Include special phone numbers such as the ready reference line, the number to use when renewing or requesting material, that of the children's department, and other often-used areas.
2. library card applications. Not everyone who attends a program has a library card. Having little ones to keep an eye on and carry may make it difficult to fill out the application while at the library. By making it available, the application can be taken home to be filled out or completed prior to entering the circulation area and simply dropped off.
3. information on how to connect with your library online if it is on the Internet. Give your Web page address and if possible include a help-line number where a patron can obtain assistance.
4. your business card if you have one. Contact names are important not only to personalize your services but also to help people feel more comfortable in the library. Some people may be intimidated by libraries, and if they have someone's name they may be less likely to hesitate to come in or call.
5. newsletters of publications that your library or facility may have. This helps the patron become aware of what the library is already doing—not only in their interest area but beyond it as well.

Guidelines or a welcoming sheet can help the group understand what is going to happen during the program, and what is expected of the children and adults participating. These guidelines can take up an entire sheet of paper, be included on another handout, or posted on signs or posters where all can see them, as well as incorporated into the presenter's introduction. It does help create a more relaxed atmosphere when the adults understand the kind of behavior the presenter expects from the children and the adults. If possible, the developmental stages for this age group may prove enlightening for the adult in terms of what to expect of the child's growth.

Many adults feel they must say all the words to a rhyme correctly, but have a hard time remembering everything that was said or done during a program or the exact words to a specific rhyme—even though children this age don't mind if some of the words are not the "authentic" ones. Creating a sheet with the most frequently used rhymes on it is useful and can be used again and again. If you prefer theme programs, you can create a sheet with just the rhymes that reflect the theme. Suggested audiotapes or CDs that have rhyme, fingerplays, and songs can be added to these sheets, also. An easy handout could be the words to a fingerplay or song with the outline of a fingerpuppet to use with it. See Figures 5-1 and 5-2 in Appendix C for samples and resources. You could also create a handout in the shape of, for example, an apple and print the words to the fingerplay "Two Little Apples" on it to remind the participants of the rhyme at home.

Very young children learn in many ways. They use all of their senses to explore their world and to develop their skills. Arts-and-crafts recipes on a handout can help the adults with limited time and funds to be "creative" so they will not feel the lack of the more expensive educational or elaborate toys on the market. This handout does not have to have every recipe; instead include a few very simple and safe ones, then supply the participants with additional resources they can look to for more arts-and-crafts ideas. If your time is really tight, look around to see what you have available in house. Are there extra book jackets lying around? Take them to your program and give suggestions on what to do with them, such as creating posters for the back of the child's door, changing table, eating, or quiet area or making them into placemats for the child's highchair. Picture cards can be made by pasting pictures from the book jackets on index cards and then covering them with clear contact paper. Encourage a dialog between the adult and child to talk about what the picture depicts, perhaps even checking out the book it is from. This kind of handout involves both the adult and child to share an experience and helps bring stories and books into the daily lives of busy families.

Program outlines and materials used can be a review sheet for adult participants. Bibliographies of recommended books for the 12-to-24-month age group can guide them in selecting books for children this age. Such bibliographies should include resources they might find useful to reinforce the language-sharing experience with their child.

Handouts that aid in the adult's understanding of child development and situations are another good idea. These can comprise a list of stages of development the child must go through, reasons to read to their child and its benefits, and/or parenting tips. Helping the adult identify developmental stages and stressing the fact that each child develops at his or her own pace can emphasize the importance of the process of developing and the important role of adult interaction and language.

Evaluation handouts help you get feedback for your program, which enables you not only to examine and assess your program but also to decide priorities for programming. The written support and comments of adults who want this kind of language experience is important. The evaluation needs to include some basic questions: How old is your child? What did you like best/least about the program? Have you used any of the ideas/materials at home? Was the time relatively convenient? Suggestions and/or comments should be welcome. Two examples of evaluations are included in Figures 5-3 and 5-4 in Appendix C.

Handouts don't need to be elaborate. Booklists may already be in existence, guides to your collection may also be available. Your library may receive distribution copies of newspapers or magazines aimed at adults working with this age group or parents. Remember to include park district activity booklets, community college offerings, and farm guides. These handouts help adults become aware of library and community services around them that they can share with their child or children.

Other agencies also offer handout materials encouraging adults to read to the very young child or information related to parenting. The American Library Association, the National Association for the Education of Young Children, and other groups have handouts that can be purchased. Check their Websites for offerings.

Figures 5-5 to 5-10 in Appendix C are sample handouts. These can be used as is, adapted for your own needs, or simply serve as idea starters for your own work. Remember to include library/facility identification information on them. Room has been left for you to add details such as clip art, stickers, stamps, and other decorations. Be aware of copyright laws and restrictions when using patterns and artwork other than your own. Many computer programs also supply decorative artwork such as Microsoft Publisher, Word, ClipArt, and Print Shop. Books with reproducible borders and artwork can be found in book stores and school supply stores if cut and paste is your method of creating handouts.

RESOURCES FOR HANDOUTS

Publishers

Copycat
  P.O. Box 081546
  Racine, WI 53408-1546
  414-634-0146
  www.copycatpress.com

Dover Publications, Inc.
31 E. 2nd Street
Mineola, New York 11501

Ellison Educational Equipment
P.O. Box 8309
Newport Beach, CA 92658-8209
800-253-2238
www.ellison.com

The Good Apple Book of Reproducible Patterns: A Colossal Collection of Captivating Images, by Nancee McClure (1991). Available from:
Good Apple
299 Jefferson Rd.
P.O. Box 480
Parsippany, NJ 07054-0480

Kidstamps
P.O. Box 18699
Cleveland Heights, OH 44118
800-727-5437
www.kidstamps.com

Lollipops Magazine for Preschool and Early Childhood Educators
Good Apple
P.O. Box 37396
Boone, IA 50037-4396
800-264-9873

Totline
Frank Shaffer Publications
23740 Hawthorne Blvd
Torrance, CA 90505-5927
800-421-5533
www.frankschaffer.com/totline.html

Clip art
This material can be found in the form of software, actual books, and online. A name to know is:

Libraries Unlimited
P.O. Box 6633
Englewood, CO 80155-6633
800-237-6124
www.ul.com/lu

APPENDIX A: BIBLIOGRAPHIES

RESOURCES ON BRAIN RESEARCH

BOOKS

Bruer, John T. *The Myth of the First Three Years: A New Understanding of Early Brain Development and Lifelong Learning.* New York: Free Press, 1999.

Bruno, Frank J. *The Family Encyclopedia of Child Psychology and Development.* New York: John Wiley, 1992.

Carnegie Task Force on Meeting the Needs of Young Children. *Starting Points: Meeting the Needs of Our Youngest Children: The Report of the Carnegie Task Force on Meeting the Needs of Young Children.* New York: Carnegie Corporation of New York.

Eliot, Lise. *What's Going on in There? How the Brain and Mind Develop in the First Five Years of Life.* New York: Bantam, 1999.

Golinkoff, Roberta Michnick, and Kathy Hirsh-Pasek. *How Babies Talk: The Magic and Mystery of Language in the First Three Years of Life.* New York: Dutton, 1999.

Gopnik, Alison, Andrew N. Meltzoff, and Patricia Kuhl. *The Scientist in the Crib: Minds, Brains, and How Children Learn.* New York: Morrow, 1999.

Healy, Jane. M. *Your Child's Growing Mind: A Guide to Learning and Brain Development from Birth to Adolescence.* Rev. ed. New York: Doubleday, 1994.

Kotulak, Ronald. *Inside the Brain: Revolutionary Discoveries of How the Mind Works.* Kansas City, Mo.: Andrews and McMeel, 1996.

Staso, William H. *Brain under Construction: Experiences that Promote the Intellectual Capabilities of Young Toddlers.* Book 2 of a series: *6–18 months.* Orcutt, Calif.: Great Beginnings, 1997.

ARTICLES

"Brain Development Is Remarkable during First Few Years." *USA Today* (August 1999): 8.

"Brain Research Finds and Suggested Actions." Oregon's Child: Everyone's Business, Straight Shooting Exhibit, Oregon State Capital (February 1997).

Mathews, Virginia H. *Kids Can't Wait . . . Library Advocacy Now!* President's Paper for Mary R. Somerville, president, 1996–97, ALA.

Muha, Laura. "Your Baby's Amazing Brain." *Parenting* (fall 1999).

Puckett, Margaret, Carol Sue Marshall, and Ruth Davis. "Examining the Emergence of Brain Development Research: The Promises and the Perils." *Childhood Education* (fall 1999): 8–12.

Simmons, Tim, and Ruth Sheehan. "Brain Research Manifests Importance of First Years." *News & Observer* (February 16, 1997). Available online at *www.news-observer.com/2little2late/stories/day1-main.html.*

WEBSITES

www.nncc.org/wh/whconf.html
The White House Conference on Early Childhood Development and Learning. April 17, 1997. Contains links to other Websites on the latest in brain research.

www.nccic.org/cctopics/brain.html
National Child Care Information Center. Provides an overview of the resources available. Lists publications in addition to organizations and provides links to information on brain development in infants and toddlers for parents and caregivers. (Does not endorse listings.)

www.hpl.lib.tx.us/events/hdr_index.html
Houston Public Library's 1998 Harriet Dickson Reynold Program "BabyThink: Babies Belong in the Library" page. Has extensive list of Internet links covering fact sheets, articles, libraries, programs, and organizations, including the American Library Association, that relate to brain development and other areas concerning the very young child and the library.

www.nap.edu/htm/sor
National Research Council containing report from the Colorado Department of Education "Starting Out Right: A Guide to Promoting Children's Reading Success" (ISBN 0-309-06410-4). Print version available though the National Academy Press (800-624-6242). Available online at *http://stills.nap.edu/html/sor.*

www.lili.org/isl/rlbrain.htm
Idaho Library Association's brain-development page. Includes implications of such research for librarians, parents, and caregivers; facts and links for more information about brain development. Excellent bibliography listing brain-development materials.

www.iamyourchild.org
I Am Your Child homepage. Information about brain research, child development ages zero to three years, resources, and more.

www.naeyc.org/resources/eyly/1997/11htm
National Association for the Education of Young Children. Early years are learning years: what it means for young children and their families.

www.ecnewsnet.org
Chicago Early Childhood News Network—Brain Research. Go to

"Brainlinks" section for links to the following: Early Childhood Initiative at the University of Chicago, Erikson Institute, Zero to Three Infant Development and Education, Society for Research In Child Development, San Francisco Early Childhood Information System Network.

www.nncc.org

National Network for Child Care. Serving professionals and families who care for children and youth. Select "Information Station," next "Child Development," then "Brain Development."

www.governor.wa.gov/early/home1.htm

The Governor's Commission on Early Learning. Gov. Gary Locke, state of Washington. January 2000.

RESOURCES FOR CHILD DEVELOPMENT

BOOKS

Ames, Louise Bates. *Your One-Year-Old: The Fun Loving, Fussy 12–24 month old*. New York: Dell, 1982.

Bos, Bev. *Before the Basics: Creating Conversations with Children*. Roseville, Calif: Turn-the-Page Press, 1983.

Caplan, Frank and Theresa. *The Second Twelve Months of Life*. New York: Putnam, 1977.

Eisenberg, Arlene, Heidi Murkoff, and Sandee E. Hathaway. *What to Expect: The Toddler Years*. New York: Workman, 1994.

Ernst, Linda L. *Lapsit Services for the Very Young: A How-to-Do-It Manual*. New York: Neal-Schuman, 1995.

Golinkoff, Roberta Michnick, and Kathy Hirsh-Pasek. *How Babies Talk: The Magic and Mystery of Language in the First Three Years of Life*. New York: Dutton, 1999.

Herb, Steven, and Sara Willoughby-Herb. *Using Children's Books in Preschool Settings: A How-to-Do-It Manual for School and Public Librarians*. New York: Neal-Schuman, 1994.

Hobbs, Sylvia. *Parent Handbook for Pretoddler Observation Class*. Bellevue, Wash.: Bellevue Community College, 1987.

Kutner, Lawrence. *Toddlers and Preschoolers: A Parent and Child Series*. New York: Morrow, 1994.

Mathews, Virginia H., and Susan Roman. *The Library-Museum Head Start Partnership*. Washington, D.C.: Center for the Book in the Library of Congress, 1999.

Nespeca, Sue McCleaf. *Library Programming for Families with Young Children: A How-to-Do-It Manual*. New York: Neal-Schuman, 1994.

Van der Zande, Irene. *1,2,3 . . . The Toddler Years: A Practical Guide for Parents and Caregivers*. Santa Cruz, Calif.: Toddler Care Center, 1993.

VIDEOS

Washington Research Institute. *Language Is the Key: A Mulitilingual Language Building Program for Young Children. Talking and Books* and *Talking and Play*. Produced by the Washington Research Institute with Mary Maddox, Kevin Cole, and Angela Notari-Syverson. Each tape 20 minutes. Washington Research Institute, 1998, rev. 1999. Two videocassettes and manual. Currently available in English and Spanish, soon to be available in additional languages. For more information, call 206-285-9317 or online at *www.wri-edu.org/bookplay*.

WEBSITES

www.nncc.org — National Network for Child Care. This site has an "Info Station" that will direct you to articles, resources and other links.

www.iamyourchild.org — The "I Am Your Child" homepage.

www.nccic.org/cctopics — National Child Care Information Center. Covers child-care topics.

www.naeyc.org/naeyc — National Association for the Education of Young Children. "Children's Champions" links to many other sites.

www.ala.org/alsc/teachers.links.html#development — The American Library Association, the ALSC Division. Has sites for teachers, parents, and librarians. This address goes directly to the list of sites for child development.

RESOURCES FOR THE SPECIAL NEEDS CHILD

Feinberg, Sandra, Kathleen Deerr, Barbara Jordan, and Michelle Langa. *Including Families of Children with Special Needs: A How-to-Do-It Manual for Librarians*. New York: Neal-Schuman, 1999.

Greenspan, Stanley I., and Serena Wieder, with Robin Simons. *The Child with Special Needs: Encouraging Intellectual and Emotional Growth*. Reading, Mass.: Addison Wesley, 1998.

Library Service to Children with Special Needs Committee, Association for Library Service to Children. *Programming for Serving Children with Special Needs*. Chicago: American Library Association, 1994.

Wright, Kieth C., and Judith F. Davie. *Serving the Disabled: A How-to-Do-It Manual for Librarians*. New York: Neal-Schuman, 1991.

RESOURCES ON SERVICE AREAS

Ernst, Linda L. *Lapsit Services for the Very Young: A How-to-Do-It Manual*. New York: Neal-Schuman, 1995.

Feinberg, Sandra, Joan F. Kuchner, and Sari Feldman. *Learning Environments for Young Children: Rethinking Library Spaces and Services*. Chicago: American Library Association, 1998.

Feinberg, Sandra, and Kathleen Deerr. *Running a Parent/Child Workshop: A How-to-Do-It Manual for Librarians*. New York: Neal-Schuman, 1995.

Feinberg, Sandra and Sari Feldman. *Serving Families and Children through Partnerships: A How-to-Do-It Manual for Librarians*. New York: Neal-Schuman, 1996.

Lenser, Jane. *Programming for Outreach Services to Children*. Chicago: American Library Association, 1994.

Nespeca, Sue McCleaf. *Library Programming for Families with Young Children: A How-to-Do-It Manual*. New York: Neal-Schuman, 1994.

Trotta, Marcia. *Managing Library Outreach Programs: A How-to-Do-It Manual for Librarians*. New York: Neal-Schuman, 1993.

RESOURCES FOR FINGERPLAYS AND RHYMES

Briggs, Diane. *101 Fingerplays, Stories, and Songs to Use With Finger Puppets*. Chicago, Ill.: American Library Association, 1999.
This text includes books, recordings, finger puppet patterns, and fingerplays with directions. All materials are intended to be used with very young children. Puppets can be used as finger puppets, stick puppets, or as flannel-board pieces.

Chorao, Kay. *Knock at the Door and Other Baby Action Rhymes*. New York: Dutton, 1999.

This simple book presents each rhyme and illustrations on each connecting two-page spread. Includes illustrated and written directions for rhymes. This can be used during the story time.

Cole, Joanna. *The Eentsy, Weentsy Spider: Fingerplays and Action Rhymes*. New York: Mulberry Books, 1991.

Davis, Sandra Carpenter. *Bounce Me Tickle Me Hug Me: Lap Rhymes and Play Rhymes from Around the World*. Toronto: The Parent-Child Mother Goose Program, 1997.

These rhymes are printed in the original language of the rhyme, with English translations and directions.

Defty, Jeff. *Creative Fingerplays and Action Rhymes: An Index and Guide to Their Use*. Phoenix, Ariz: Oryx, 1992.

This text provides action verses for infants through older children, ESL and special needs children, a subject index, and first-line index. Also a section evaluating, selecting, and teaching action verse.

Dunn, Opal. *Hippety-Hop Hippety Hay: Growing with Rhymes from Birth to Age Three*. New York: Henry Holt, 1999.

There are one to two rhymes per page, with directions for action under the rhyme/poem. Musical scores are included in a separate chapter.

Flint Public Library. *Ring a Ring O' Roses. Stories, Games, and Fingerplays for Pre-School Children*. 10th ed. Flint, Mich.: Flint Public Library, 1996.

The 10th edition of this collection of fingerplays for preschool children. Arranged by subject and does include a first line index for easy access. Does include Spanish translations of familiar English fingerplays along with traditional Spanish fingerplays.

Gag, Wanda. *The ABC Bunny*. New York: Coward, McCann, 1933.

Glazer, Tom. *Let's Sing Fingerplays*. Tom Glazer. Scarborough, N.Y.: CMS, 1977(?). Cassette: CMSX 4688.

———. *Eye Winker, Tom Tinker, Chin Chopper: Fifty Musical Fingerplays*. Garden City, N.Y.: Doubleday, 1973, 1978.

Griego, Marot, Betsy Bucks, Sharon Gilbert, and Laurel Kimball, trans. *Tortillitas para Mama and Other Nursery Rhymes*. New York: Holt, Rinehart and Winston, 1981.

This book has rhymes in Spanish and English.

Ives, Burl. *Burl Ives Sings a Little White Duck*. Burl Ives. New York: Columbia Records, [198_?], 1974. Cassette: PCT 33183. CD CK 33183.

Jaeger, Sally. *Sally's From Wibbleton to Wobbleton*. Produced by 49 North Prods.

Distributed by Instructional Video. 40 minutes. 1998, 1999 release. ISBN 0968450806. Videocassette.

Kleiner, Lynn. *Babies Make Music*. Produced and directed by Lynn Kleiner and Dennis Devine. 52 minutes. Redondo Beach, Calif.: Music Rhapsody, 1996. ISBN 0965363619. Videocassette.

Marino, Jane, and Dorothy F. Houlihan. *Mother Goose Time*. New York: H. W. Wilson, 1992.

Martin, Bill. *Chicka Chicka Boom Boom*. New York: Simon and Schuster Books for Young Readers, 1989

Martin, Elaine. *Baby Games*. Philadelphia, Penna.: Running Press, 1988.

McGrath, Bob. *The Baby Record*. Bob McGrath and Katharine Smithrim. Racine, Wis.: Golden, 1990. Cassette: 41007 Golden; also available in CD.

————. *Songs and Games for Toddlers*. Bob McGrath and Katharine Smithrim. Cambridge, Ont.: Golden, 1990, Cassette: 41016.

Opie, Iona and Peter. *The Oxford Nursery Rhyme Book*. New York: Oxford University Press, 1955.

Orozco, Jose-Luis. *Diez Deditos: Ten Little Fingers and Other Play Rhymes and Action Songs from Latin America*. New York: Dutton, 1997.
These Spanish action rhymes and songs also include English translations. This has both written and illustrated instructions.

Palmer, Hap. *Hap Palmer Sings Classic Nursery Rhymes*. Hap Palmer. Freeport, New York: Educational Activities, 1991. Cassette: AC 646; Compact Disk: CD 646.

Playtime: Activity Songs to Share with Your Baby. Disney Babies. Burbank, Calif.: Disney, 1991. Cassette: Disney 60609-2; CD: Disney 60609-0; Booklet: 60609-4.

Prelutsky, Jack. *Read-Aloud Rhymes for the Very Young*. New York: A. Knopf, 1986.

Ra, Carol R. *Trot Trot to Boston: Play Rhymes for Baby*. New York: Lothrop, Lee and Shepard, 1987.

Raffi. *Singable Songs for the Very Young*. Raffi. University City, Calif.: Shoreline, 1976. Cassette: MCAC 10037; CD: MCJD 10037.

Scott, Anne. *The Laughing Baby: Remembering Nursery Rhymes and Reasons. Songs and Rhymes from Around the World*. New York: Bergin and Garvey, 1987.
This text includes music for the rhymes and songs, the origin of the rhyme, and instructions on how to do the action.

Sharon, Lois and Bram. *Mainly Mother Goose*. Sharon Hampson, Lois Lilienstein, and Bram Morrison. Los Angeles, Calif.: Drive Entertainment, 1994. CD: DE2-43206 Toronto, Ont.: Elephant Records; Hollywood, Calif.: A&M Records, 1984 Cassette: EC0301.

Sierra, Judy. *The Flannel Board Storytelling Book*. 2nd ed. New York: H. W. Wilson, 1997.

Stewart, Nancy. *Little Songs for Little Me*. Nancy Stewart. Mercer Island, Wash.: Friends Street Music, 1992. Available in cassette and CD with booklet.

————. *Plant a Little Seed: Songs for Growing Children*. Nancy

Stewart. Mercer Island, Wash.: Friends Street Music, 1995. Available in cassette and CD with booklet.

Watson, Clyde. *Catch Me and Kiss Me and Say It Again*. New York: Philomel, 1978.

RESOURCES FOR PROGRAMMING IDEAS

BOOKS

Cobb, Jane. *I'm a Little Teapot! Presenting Preschool Storytime*. Vancouver, Brit. Col.: Black Sheep Press, 1996.

Ernst, Linda L. *Lapsit Services for the Very Young: A How-to-Do-It Manual*. New York: Neal-Schuman, 1995.

Feinberg, Sandra, and Kathleen Deerr. *Running a Parent/Child Workshop: A How-to-Do-It Manual for Librarians*. New York: Neal-Schuman, 1995.

Jeffery, Debby Ann. *Literate Beginnings. Programs for Babies and Toddlers*. Chicago: American Library Association, 1995.

Marino, Jane, and Dorothy F. Houlihan. *Mother Goose Time: Library Programs for Babies and Their Caregivers*. New York: Wilson, 1992.

Nespeca, Sue McCleaf. *Library Programming for Families with Young Children: A How-to-Do-It Manual*. New York: Neal-Schuman, 1994.

Nichols, Judy. *Storytimes for Two-Year-Olds*. 2d ed. Chicago: American Library Association, 1998.

ARTICLES

Dowd, Frances Smardo, and Judith Dixon. "Successful Toddler Storytimes Based on Child Development Principles." *Public Libraries* (November/December 1996): 374–80.

Feldman, Sari, and Robert Needlman. "Take Two Board Books, and Call Me in the Morning." *School Library Journal* (June 1999): 30.

Hardman, Margaret, and Lynn Jones. "Sharing Books with Babies: Evaluation of an Early Literacy Intervention." *Educational Review* (November 1999): 221–29.

Knoth, Maeve Visser. "Reading Aloud to Very Young Children." *Book Links* (July 1998): 22–24.

Kupetz, Barbara N. "A Shared Responsibility: Nurturing Literacy in the Very Young." *School Library Journal* (July 1993): 28–31.

Kupetz, Barbara N., and Elise Jepson Green. "Sharing Books with Infants and Toddlers: Facing the Challenges." *Young Children* (January 1997): 22–27.

Nespeca, Sue McCleaf. "Bringing Up Baby." *School Library Journal* (November 1999): 49–52.

Soundy, Cathleen S. "Nurturing Literacy with Infants and Toddlers in Group Settings." *Childhood Education* (spring 1997): 149–55.

Teale, William H. "Libraries Promote Early Literacy Learning: Ideas from Current Research and Early Childhood Programs." *JOYS* (spring 1999): 9–18.

RESOURCES FOR MUSIC

Bayless, Kathleen and Marjorie Ramsey. *Music: A Way of Life for the Young Child.* 4th ed. New York: Merrill, 1991.

Briggs, Diane. *101 Fingerplays, Stories, and Songs to Use with Finger Puppets.* Chicago: American Library Association, 1999.

Chadha, Nisha. *Multicultural Book of Songs.* London: Mantra, 1994.

Chorao, Kay. *Knock at the Door and Other Baby Action Rhymes.* New York: Dutton, 1999.

Davis, Sandra Carpenter. *Bounce Me Tickle Me Hug Me: Lap Rhymes and Play Rhymes from Around the World.* Toronto: Parent-Child Mother Goose Program, 1997.

Defty, Jeff. *Creative Fingerplays and Action Rhymes: An Index and Guide to Their Use.* Phoenix, Ariz.: Oryx, 1992.

Dunn, Opal. *Hippety-Hop, Hippety Hay! Growing with Rhymes from Birth to Age Three.* New York: Henry Holt, 1999.

Glazer, Tom. *Music for Ones and Twos*: Songs and Games for the Very Young Child. New York: Doubleday, 1983.

Griego, Margot, et al., sel. and trans. *Tortillitas Para Mama and Other Nursery Rhymes: Spanish and English..* New York: Henry Holt, 1981.

Jaeger, Sally. *Sally's From Wibbleton to Wobbleton.* Video, 40 minutes. 49 North Productions, Toronto, 1998.

Kleiner, Lynn, and Dennis Devine, prods. and dirs. *Babies Make Music.* Video, 52 minutes. Music Rhapsody, Redondo Beach, Calif., 1996.

Orozco, Jose-Luis. *Diez Deditos: Ten Little Fingers and Other Play Rhymes and Action Songs from Latin America.* New York: Dutton, 1997.

Palmer, Hap. *Baby Songs.* Video, 30 mins. Los Angeles: Hi-Tops Video, 1987

Reid, Rob. *Children's Jukebox: A Subject Guide to Musical Recordings and Programming Ideas for Songsters Ages One to Twelve.* Chicago: American Library Association, 1995.

Sale, Laurie. *Growing Up with Music: A Guide to the Best Recorded Music for Children*. New York: Avon, 1992.

Scott, Anne. *The Laughing Baby: Remembering Nursery Rhymes and Reasons. Songs and Rhymes from Around the World*. New York: Bergin and Garvey, 1987.

Silberg, Jackie. *Games to Play with Toddlers*. Beltsville, Md.: Gryphon House, 1993.

—————. *I Can't Sing Book for Grownups Who Can't Carry a Tune in a Paper Bag . . . But Want to Do Music with Young Children*. Beltsville, Md.: Gryphon House, 1998.

Stewart, Nancy. *Little Songs for Little Me*. Sound recording. Friends Street Music, 1992.

—————. *Plant a Little Seed: Songs for Growing Children*. Sound recording. Friends Street Music, 1995.

WEBSITES

www.bestchildrensmusic.com	Gives reviews of recordings.
www.funmusicideas.com	Advice and links to other sites, free monthly newsletter.
www.childrensmusic.org	Children's Music Web. A non-profit organization dedicated to music for kids, has ties with other related organizations such as Children's Music Network. Covers research on music and the brain.
www.comnonline.org	Children's Music Network
www.childrensmusichouse.com	Children's Music House began as a distributor in 1980 serving public libraries and schools. Supplies recorded music, videos, audiobooks, read alongs, and DVDs.
www.kimboed.com	Kimbo
www.2-life.com/meyc	Music Education for Young Children Website
www.nancymusic.com/index.htm	Friends Street Music
www.musicrhapsody.com	Music Rhapsody
members.tripod.com/~ESL4Kids	The EFL Playhouse. A resource for teachers of young learners. Information about working with ESL families and materials to use.

RESOURCES FOR FLANNEL BOARDS

Carlson, Ann, and Mary Carlson. *Flannelboard Stories for Infants and Toddlers*. Chicago: American Library Association, 1999.

Sierra, Judy. *The Flannel Board Storytelling Book*. 2nd ed. New York: Wilson, 1997.

RESOURCES FOR PUPPETS

Briggs, Diane. *101 Fingerplays, Stories and Songs to Use with Finger Puppets*. Chicago: American Library Association, 1999.

Hunt, Tamara, and Nancy Renfro. *Pocketful of Puppets: Mother Goose*. Austin, Tex.: Nancy Renfro Studios, 1982.

————. *Puppetry in Early Childhood Education*. Austin, Tex.: Nancy Renfro Studios, 1982.

Rottman, Fran. *Easy-to-Make Puppets and How to Use Them*. Ventura, Calif.: Gospel Light, 1995.

RESOURCES FOR ACTIVITIES

Catlin, Cynthia. *More Toddlers Together: The Complete Planning Guide for a Toddler Curriculum*. Vol. 2. Beltsville, Md.: Gryphon House, 1996.

————. *Toddlers Together*. Beltsville, Md.: Gryphon House, 1994.

Hodges, Susan. *Toddler Art*. Torrance, Calif.: Totline, 1998.

Kohl, MaryAnn F. *Mudworks: Creative Clay, Dough and Modeling Experiences*. Bellingham, Wash.: Bright Ring, 1989.

Martin, Elaine. *Baby Games*. Philadelphia, Penna.: Running Press, 1988.

Miller, Karen. *More Things to Do with Toddlers and Twos*. Chelsea, Mass.: TelShare, 1994.

————. *Things to Do with Toddlers and Twos*. Chelsea, Mass: TelShare, 1984.

Silberg, Jackie. *Games to Play with Babies*. Rev. and exp. ed. Beltsville, Md.: Gryphon House, 1993.

————. *Games to Play with Toddlers*. Beltsville, Md.: Gryphon House, 1993.

Staso, William H. *Brain under Construction: Experiences That Promote the Intellectual Capabilities of Young Toddlers.* Book 2 of a series: *8–18 months.* Orcutt, Calif.: Great Beginnings, 1997.

APPENDIX B: ACRONYMS AND AGENCIES

Here are some acronyms that you should know

Acronym	Name	Website
ALA	American Library Association	www.ala.org
ALSC	Association for Library Services to Children	www.ala.org/alsc
CBLC	The Center for the Book in the Library of Congress	www.loc.gov/loc/ cfbook
EHS NRC	Early Head Start National Resource Center	www.ehsnrc.org
ERICEECE	ERIC Clearinghouse on Elementary and Early Childhood Education	http://ericeece.org
IAYC	I Am Your Child	www.iamyourchild.org
MOMS	Moms Offering Moms Support	www.momsclub.org
MOPS	Mothers of Preschoolers	www.gospelcom.net/ mops/
NACCRRA	National Association of Child Care Resources and Referral Agencies	www.naccrra.net
NAEYC	National Association for the Education of the Young Child	www.naeyc.org

Acronym	Name	Website
NCCIC	National Child Care Information Center	*http://nccic.org*
NHSA	National Head Start Association	*www.nhsa.org*
NNCC	National Network for Child Care	*www.nncc.org*
PCHP	Parent-Child Home Program (formerly Mother-Child Home Program)	*www.parent-child.org*
PEPS	Program for Early Parent Support	*www.newhorizons. org/ofc_peps.html*
U.S. Dept.Ed.	United States Department of Education	*www.ed.gov* (Use the SEARCH button)
Zero to Three	Zero to Three	*www.zerotothree.org*

APPENDIX C:
HANDOUTS

Figure 4–1. Welcome and Guidelines

Welcome Everybody – How Do You Do?!

This is a special library time just for you!

Here are a few "rules" to keep in mind when our program is in session. Your cooperation will help everyone to enjoy and profit from these programs.

1. Parent participation is key to the success of this program. You are best equipped to help your child focus on our activities. Please join in and show your child how much fun it is!

2. Please put toys and food away. They distract your child and others. If bottles, blankets or other "not-to-be-parted with items" are necessary, we will work with it. Breastfeeding is also okay if need be.

3. You will probably have lots to share with the other adults. Time for this has been made after the program. We would like to do the activities first, while the children are fresh. The room is booked for your use afterwards.

4. If your child is crying loudly or otherwise distracting the group, or in another sense "losing it," please feel free to step out for a moment and regroup. Talk to me if you are unsure or concerned about your child's behavior.

5. RELAX! It is not expected that your child will sit still and participate in each activity. Our goal is to have fun with rhymes, song, books, and other language-building play.

THANKS FOR BEING HERE!

Figure 4–2. Sample Guidelines Handouts

The two items below are sample guidelines you can use when making your own handouts.

Just a reminder . . .

Story time for this age group lasts about 20 minutes. Please be on time.

Please put away all food and toys before we start.

If your child seems over-whelmed or unhappy, please feel free to step outside or try again an-other time.

Set a good example for your child with your par-ticipation.

Relax and have fun!

Welcome to a special story time just for you and your child.

So everyone has a great time, please remember:

YOU are the key. Please join in and show your child it's fun!

Please put distractions away for now, if possible. No food, bottles, etc. If absolutely needed, be discreet.

Having a rough day? Step outside for a moment, or if need be try again another day.

There's lots to share, so let's save personal conversations for before or after program when there is lots of time.

Most of all, ENOY this special time with your child.

Figure 5–1. Flannel Board Handout

FLANNEL BOARD FUN

Flannel boards or felt boards are interactive, and children love to play with them. They can develop along with your child in the complexity of the pieces. Children can practice their motor skills while having fun putting pieces on the board. Keep it simple at this young age so your child will feel success when involved with it, be it by simply putting pieces on and off or while you recite a rhyme.

Felt, flannel, or peplum may be used.

Backing: Material can be cut to size to fit a piece of cardboard that can be inserted into a large "zippered" bag, the inside top cover of an individual pizza box, or the inside lid of a shoebox. Glue down securely, and if necessary tape around edges.

Pieces can be simple cut-out shapes (circles, squares, triangles, and similar), or figures of a story/rhyme/song. They should be large enough for your child to hold and still fix on board. Use fun bright colors.

Store pieces inside box or bag.

Try *Brown Bear, Brown Bear* by Bill Martin and the nursery rhyme "Two Little Blackbirds" to get you started. Get more ideas from *The Flannel Board Storytelling Book* (Judy Sierra) and *Little Songs for Little Me* (Stewart).

Figure 5–2. Fingerpuppet Handout

GOING TO THE ZOO

An elephant goes
Like this and that.
*(hold hands together in
front of body
& swing back and forth)*
He's terrible big,
(hold hands above head)
And he's terrible fat.
(clasp hands together in front)

He has no fingers,
(wiggle fingers)
He has no toes.
(touch toes)
But goodness, gracious!
(put hands on cheeks in surprise)
What a nose!
*(hands together & swing
like trunk)*

Finger
hole

ELEPHANT PATTERN

Easy to Make Puppets by Fran Rottman. Copyright 1995.
Used by Permission

Figure 5–3. Sample Evaluation Form #1

Please let us know what you think. Fill out the evaluation below. Thanks!

1. How old is your child?

2. How many programs did you and your child attend?

3. What did you like best about the program?

4. What did you like least about the program?

5. Did it meet your expectations?

6. Have you used any of the ideas presented at home?

7. Did you think the materials were suitable for the age range?

8. Was the time relatively convenient?

9. If offered again, would you attend this class?

10. Suggestions and/or comments:

Figure 5–4. Sample Evaluation Form #2

Story Time for the Very Young
Please return. Thank you!

1. How did you find out about this story time?

2. What is your zip code?

3. How old is your child, in months?

4. How many programs like this have you attended at this location?

5. Have you attended story times at other locations? If so, where and how many?

6. If you bring another child or sibling as well, how old is that child?

7. What do you like best about this story time?

8. What do you like least about this story time?

9. Can you give us an example of a story, song, rhyme, or activity that has carried over from story time to home?

10. How does this program meet, or not meet, your expectations for a developmentally appropriate activity?

11. How can we improve this program for you and your child?

Figure 5–5. Fingerplays Handout

Fingerplays and Rhymes

OPEN, SHUT THEM
Open, shut them. Open, shut them.
Give a little clap!
Open, shut them. Open, shut them.
Put them in your lap.

HICKORY, DICKORY DOCK
Hickory, dickory dock.
The mouse ran up the clock.
The clock struck one,
The mouse ran down.
Hickory, dickory dock.

HERE'S A BALL FOR BABY
Here's a ball for baby,
Big and soft and round.
Here is baby's hammer,
See how he can pound.
Here are baby's soldiers,
Standing in a row.
Here is baby's music,
Clapping, clapping so.
Here is baby's trumpet,
Toot-toole-toot-toot-too.
Here's the way that baby
Plays at peek-a-boo.
Here's a big umbrella,
To keep the baby dry.
Here is baby's cradle,
Rock-a-baby bye.

ROUND AND ROUND
Round and round the garden
Goes the Teddy Bear.
One step, two step,
Tickle him under there!

MOTHER AND FATHER AND UNCLE JOHN
Mother and Father and Uncle John
Went to town, one by one.
Mother fell off......
Father fell off.......
But Uncle John went on and on and on
 and on and on...

TO MARKET, TO MARKET
To market, to market,
To buy a fat pig.
Home again, home again,
Jiggety jig.
To market, to market,
To buy a fat hog.
Home again, home again,
Jiggety jog.

CRISS CROSS APPLESAUCE
Criss cross,
 (trace X on child's back)
 Applesauce.
 (tap child's shoulders)
Spiders crawling up your back.
 (walk fingers up child's back)
Cool breeze
 (blow gently on child's neck)
Tight squeeze
 (hug child)
Now you've got the shivers!
 (tickle child)

CUP OF TEA
Here is a cup,
And here is a cup.
And here is a pot of tea.
Pour a cup, and pour a cup.
And have a cup with me!

LITTLE TURTLE
There was a little turtle,
He lived in a box.
He swam in a puddle,
He climbed on the rocks.
He snapped at a mosquito.
He snapped at a flea.
He snapped at a minnow.
He snapped at me!
He caught the mosquito.
He caught the flea.
He caught the minnow.
But he didn't catch me!

JACK IN THE BOX
Jack in the box, you sit so still.
Won't you come out?
YES, I will!

Figure 5–6. Art Recipes Handout

Art Activity Recipes

Children in this age group can be very creative. Because many children still put things in their mouths, however, it is better not to use recipes that demand a great deal of salt, the use of tempera as a coloring agent, or have alum as an ingredient. Here are some simple and fast art recipes for you to try.

Playdough
1 cup flour
1/2 cup salt
2 teaspoons cream of tartar

Mix these together and add to 1 cup of boiling water, 2 teaspoons oil, and food coloring. Cook, stirring constantly, over medium heat for 3 to 4 minutes until it forms a ball. Store in a plastic bag or sealed container. Keeps well in refrigerator.

Playdough
(This dough is firmer and holds its shape better)
4 cups of flour
1 cup salt
4 tablespoons of cooking oil or shortening
1 1/2 cups of water (if needed, add more a little at a time)
Food coloring (about 1 fluid ounce for dark color) or powdered tempera paint

Add food coloring to water for ease in mixing. If tempera is used, mix with flour and salt. Mix dry ingredients together and add liquid until pliable, somewhat like a pie crust. Stored in a plastic bag, this will keep for about a month, depending on use. If it gets too sticky, just add more flour.

Oatmeal Dough
1 cup flour
2 cups oatmeal
1 cup water

Cook mixed ingredients over medium heat, stirring constantly for 3 minutes. Knead well. When cool, store in plastic bag with tight seal.

Glue or Cornstarch Paste
One of the simplest pastes to make is a mixture of flour and cold water. It does not keep well, so make small amounts at a time. For colored paste, add food coloring.
Cornstarch paste is made by mixing 3 tablespoons of cornstarch in 1 cup of cold water, and boiling the mixture until it thickens. When it is cool, it can be used as paste. This separates over time, so reheat and cool before using again.

Fingerpaint
Children love to use fingerpaint and really get involved with it. If you prefer, use food as fingerpaint for your very young child. Applesauce, yogurt, canned pumpkin, sour cream, and cranberry sauce are only a few ideas to start with, then use your imagination. To make fingerpaint you may also use this recipe: 1/2 cup cornstarch and 3/4 cup cold water. Bring to boil in a pot. Add 2 cups of boiling water that has food coloring already added to it. Cook until it boils clear. Cool mixture and then use.

Figure 5–7. Craft Ideas Handout

Craft Ideas

It's fun to make things for you and your child to play with and enjoy together. Here are a few ideas.

Stick Puppets
Use a craft stick, ice cream stick, tongue depressor, or even a wooden spoon. Cut a circle out of colored paper, tape it on one end of the stick, and decorate. Use stickers or draw on a face.

Picture Cards
Use unlined index cards. Glue pictures from magazines, decorative stickers, or even photographs you've taken to the card. Using clear contact paper, place the decorated side of the index card face down on the sticky side. Covering both sides helps durability of card. Sort into dishpan or box, which can also be used for storage.

Can Lids
Cleaned juice lids from frozen juice cans are great for "mailing" into a coffee can with a hole cut in the top. Lids can be decorated with stickers or used as is. Makes a great sound.

Squish Bags
Pudding — In a bowl combine contents of 1 box of instant pudding mix with about 1/2 to 3/4 amount of water usually required. Chocolate makes great "dirt," or add food coloring to vanilla pudding. Mix well. Put about 1/4 cup of mixture into a zip-lock bag, press out as much air as possible, and seal well.

Cream Bags
Use whipped cream or shaving cream (if your child has stopped chewing on every-thing). Fill a zip-lock plastic bag about 1/2 full. Add a few drops of food coloring. Seal well and squeeze to mix.
Note: Freezer bags work the best since they are the strongest. Taping the opening end shut helps keep them that way when children play with them.

Books
You can make books that follow your child through his or her day, on things that go, a trip to the farm, favorite things, and the like. Glue pictures on lightweight tag board or construction paper. Insert into plastic page protectors or cover both sides with clear contact paper. You will need to punch holes to fasten them together if not using page protectors. Join the pages together in a three ring binder, use ring fasteners, or tie with yarn. This gives your child his or her very personal book. You can even create a book from plastic bags, cutting cardboard to fit and then drawing or gluing on pictures, sew-ing the bags together with yarn.

Figure 5–8. Water Theme Handout

All Wet!

Row, Row, Row Your Boat
Row, row, row your boat,
Gently down the stream.
Merrily, merrily, merrily, merrily,
Life is but a dream.

1-2-3-4-5, I Caught a Fish Alive
One, two, three, four, five,
I caught a fish alive!
Six, seven, eight, nine, ten,
I let it go again!

Rub A Dub Dub
Rub-a-dub-dub, three men in a tub,
And who do you think they be?
The butcher, the baker, the candlestick maker
And all of them gone to sea.

More Ideas!

Put out a small pan of water and let your child wash some dishes or perhaps a baby doll. Children this age love to imitate the big people around them.

Take a walk around a pond, lake, or stream in your area. Talk about what you see and hear.

Sand is lots of fun for little ones and it is best kept outside. You can use a simple dishpan or dump it in a box. Be sure to supply containers and digging equipment.

Bubbles can add a smile to any day. Put on some music and dance with your child amid this bubbly fun. Best done outside or in a room that won't get damaged by moisture.

Books
Picturebooks to share with your child!

In the Small, Small Pond by Fleming.
Little Elephant photos by Hoban.
Splash! by McDonnell
Have You Seen My Duckling? by Tafuri

Figure 5–9. Parent Education Handout

Reading Aloud to Little Ones

Things to remember:

It starts with YOU!
Let your child see you reading at home.
Have reading materials around the house.
Make the time to share a story, rhyme, or any positive language experience with your child.
Talk to your child about what is going on around you two.
Have fun with language, and read with expression.
Make the moment a comfortable one for you and your child.
Let your child see how special books are by the way you handle them.

When selecting books remember:

Pick stories you like to hear because you'll end up reading them again and again.
Encourage your child to point to the pictures and talk about them together.
Select stories that have rhythm.
Look for artwork that is bright and clear, with white space for resting the eye.

Remember your little one:

May like to select the story.
May only listen to a little at first, but will get better.
Needs the adult to share the book with, otherwise it's just a toy.

Stories to Share.

Big Fat Hen — Baker
Barnyard Tracks — Duffy
Little Robin Red Breast — Halpern
Where's Spot? — Hill
I Hear — Isadora
Brown Bear, Brown Bear — Martin
Clap Hands — Oxenbury
On Mother's Lap — Scott
"More, More, More," Said the Baby — Williams
Little Mouse, the Red Ripe Strawberry and the Big Hungry Bear — Wood

Figure 5–10. Things That Go Handout

Things That Go

Rhymes/Songs

To Market, To Market
Bumping Downtown in My Little Red
Wagon
Wheels on the Bus
Down by the Station
Row, Row, Row Your Boat
I've Been Working on the Railroad

Books

Freight Train - Crews
I Love Boats — McDonnell
Sheep in a Jeep — Shaw
Chugga-Chugga Choo-Choo — Lewis

Things to do!

Use a large laundry basket as a vehicle—
car, boat, train—and let
your child "go somewhere."

Give your child a box or laundry
basket to push with a doll
or toy inside, and move it
from one place to another.

While driving, play tour guide
for your child and describe
what you see.

Use a magnetic picture album
and pictures in magazines to
create a book about "things that go."

Take a bus or ferry ride.

Remember to take along
foods/drinks that can go, too!

Figure 5–11. Sign Suggestions

Sign suggestions:

Sorry
This program may only last 20 minutes since the children are very young and have a short attention span.

Story Time has already started. *Please* wait until there is a pause in the program and I will let you in. *Thanks!*

CHECK THESE OUT!

Please remember:
*Get involved with what we are doing.
*Snacks & toys away for now.
*Time for sharing after the program.

Welcome to Story Time!

My name is

_____

GENERAL INDEX

INDEX OF PICTURE BOOK AUTHORS

INDEX OF PICTURE BOOK TITLES

INDEX OF FIRST LINES FOR RHYMES, FINGERPLAYS AND SONGS

INDEX OF THEMES
FOR PROGRAMS

ABOUT THE AUTHOR

Linda Ernst has been a children's librarian for the past twenty-two years. Actively serving very young children and their caregivers for the past thirteen years has been an important part of her job and one of the most enjoyable. Just as parents are encouraged to keep it simple and start early to expose their children to the world of language and literature, Ernst offers assistance in applying this knowledge to the areas of library service and programming for very young children. She has given lapsit training workshops for the King County Library System, Seattle Public Library, Everett Public Library, and the Sno-Isle Library System in Washington. She has also given workshops in Scottsdale, Arizona, and for the Washington/Idaho Library Association's Joint Conference. She has guided and encouraged adults to discover, develop, and to share the lapsit experience with very young children. The author is currently employed by the King County Library System in Washington and has served communities in Illinois and Washington. Linda L. Ernst lives in Bellevue, Washington, with her husband and daughter.

JUN 2002